Statement of Faith

The Holy Church

First Edition

Published under the imprint The Common Faith, denoting an open, ecumenical
publishing ethos oriented toward the shared inheritance of the Christian tradition.

ISBN: 979-8-9942707-0-7

Reader's Preface

This *Statement of Faith* may at first appear unusual to some readers. Not because it departs from Scripture, but because it adheres so closely to it. Not because it offers profound new ways of thinking, but because it states core beliefs—in fact, the most essential doctrines—of Christianity so plainly. What is set forth here is intentionally biblical in substance, yet not merely a collection of biblical citations or paraphrases. It reflects instead the manner in which the faith was first known, confessed, guarded, and transmitted within the life of the Church.

The doctrines articulated here are not presented as an exhaustive account of Christian teaching, but as those teachings without which the faith itself could not be recognized, confessed, or handed on. They are *constitutive* in character: doctrines whose confession and enactment bring Christian identity and worship into being, and without which the Church could not intelligibly baptize, pray, or proclaim the gospel. These are not selected for their simplicity or minimalism, but for their necessity. Remove them, and Christianity ceases to be Christianity rather than merely becoming incomplete.

The earliest Christians did not possess a completed New Testament. The apostolic writings were received gradually, copied, circulated, read aloud in worship, and recognized over time. Long before the Church could appeal to a fixed list of books, it nevertheless knew what it believed. It baptized, prayed, proclaimed, suffered, and worshiped according to a shared confession that had been received rather than invented. This pattern was not a novelty of the early Church, but stood in continuity with Israel's own reliance on spoken confession, recited law, psalmody, and remembered acts of God.

In this setting, the Church relied upon what came to be called the *Rule of Faith*—a received measure by which teaching was recognized, tested, and confessed. The word "rule" here signifies not coercion, but measure: a standard against which claims could be compared. The same term, *kanon*, would later be used to describe the canon of Scripture itself. Scripture and rule were thus not rivals, but mutually reinforcing realities. The rule did not replace the apostolic writings; it served as the living pattern by which those writings were recognized as faithful, read rightly, and preserved.

As the Church discerned which writings bore apostolic authority, several marks proved decisive: connection to the apostles or their companions, origin within the apostolic era, conformity to the received confession, and widespread use among the churches. These marks were not imposed after the fact, but reflected the Church's already-established sense of what must be held in order for the faith to remain itself. Writings that failed to conform to this measure were set aside, whether because they were late, falsely attributed, or taught a different faith. Other texts, while not received as Scripture, continued to be read for instruction or historical insight. By the fourth century, what the Church had long practiced had become stable and publicly acknowledged.

If the inspiration of Scripture is confessed, then its preservation is not unexpected. Yet that preservation did not occur only through writing. It occurred through repetition, public confession, catechesis, prayer, and worship. The Holy Spirit preserved the faith not only by guiding authors, but by forming a people capable of remembering, rehearsing, and handing on what they had received. The canon represents the textual crystallization of this apostolic deposit, not its invention.

For this reason, this *Statement of Faith* attends closely to the forms by which the most essential doctrines of the faith were made memorable and durable within the Church. Creeds, catechetical summaries, baptismal formulas, liturgical texts, lectionaries, inscriptions, and rites all served as vehicles of transmission. These forms did not attempt to say everything that could be said, but what had to be said. Their authority lay not in novelty or precision for its own sake, but in their capacity to preserve the heart of the faith through communal repetition—what could be said together, prayed together, sung together, and enacted together across generations.

The deliberate restraint of this Statement follows from this purpose. Other doctrines—normative, formative, regulative, catechetical, paraenetic, or traditional—have played vital roles in the Church's life, shaping belief, ordering practice, and forming Christian character. They are neither denied nor diminished here. Yet they do not function in the same way. They presuppose what is constitutive; they depend upon it rather than generate it. To elaborate them fully would be to change the nature of the document, shifting it from a confessional witness to a systematic account.

This Statement therefore does not seek to resolve every later controversy, nor to adjudicate questions that arose after the Church's shared confession had already taken shape. Silence on such matters is not dismissal, but discipline— an acknowledgment that not every true teaching functions as a confessional boundary, and that not every important doctrine is identity-constituting.

Nor is this Statement intended as a condemnation or devaluation of positions held by many faithful Christians in good conscience. Its aim is not to narrow the faith to a party or system, but to articulate what the Church confessed together before division. It seeks to present the faith as received—measured, remembered, and handed on—so that readers may recognize themselves not as inventors of belief, but as heirs.

What follows is therefore offered as a witness: a public articulation of those constitutive doctrines by which the Church learned to confess the gospel, guard its teaching, and remain one in faith across time. It is set forth to orient the reader, not to replace Scripture; to clarify confession, not to supplant inquiry; and to locate belief within the shared memory of the people of God.

Authority Statement:
Proemium & Ecclesial Voice

The faith confessed by the Church did not arise from private reflection, nor was it assembled by later agreement. It was received: first proclaimed in the mighty acts of God, borne by the apostles in word and deed, entrusted to the churches, and preserved through common confession, prayer, and practice. Before it was written, it was believed; before it was defined, it was lived; before it was disputed, it was worshiped. Accordingly, this Statement of Faith speaks in the voice of the Church. It does not proceed from an individual author, nor from private judgment, nor from a school, party, sect, branch, denomination, or ecclesial family within the household of faith. The "we" by which it speaks is the corporate voice of the faithful gathered in continuity with the apostles: the Church believing what she has received, confessing what she has been taught, and bearing witness to the truth entrusted to her care.

When this Statement declares, "We believe," it echoes the baptismal confession by which believers are incorporated into Christ and sealed into the Church, confessed in interrogatory form and answered in faith (the *Didache* 7; *Apostolic Tradition* [baptismal interrogations]). When it says, "We confess," it stands with the martyrs and teachers who named the truth under trial, and with the councils that rendered public and binding testimony to the apostolic proclamation (Nicaea 325; Constantinople 381; Chalcedon 451). When it proceeds in ordered exposition, it follows the ancient catechetical pattern by which a received confession is explained so that it may be confessed with understanding—without being altered by explanation (Cyril of Jerusalem, *Catechetical Lectures* [*Catecheses*]; Ambrose of Milan, *On the Sacraments* [*De Sacramentis*]; Augustine of Hippo, *On the Catechizing of the Uninstructed* [*De catechizandis rudibus*]).

In the centuries prior to the great division of the Church, what later generations would call a "statement of faith" did not ordinarily appear as a single, independent document. Yet the Church was never without such statements in substance and function. From the earliest period, she lived by a rule of faith (*regula fidei*, κανὼν τῆς πίστεως): a received summary of the apostolic teaching, confessed before Scripture was interpreted and guarding how Scripture was to be read. Thus Irenaeus speaks of a rule "received from the apostles and their disciples," confessed with one and the same substance across the churches scattered throughout the world (Irenaeus of Lyons, *Against Heresies* [*Adversus Haereses*] I.10.1–2; III.4.1). Tertullian treats this same rule as fixed and prior, the boundary of faithful teaching and the measure by which novelty is judged (Tertullian, *On the Prescription of Heretics* [*De Praescriptione Haereticorum*] 13, 21, 37).

Justin Martyr likewise presupposes stable doctrinal content confessed at baptism and rehearsed in the assembly, prior to theological speculation and inseparable from worship itself (Justin Martyr, *First Apology* [*Apologia I*] 13; 61; 65–67). This confession was not merely spoken about God but spoken to God and enacted before him. In baptism, the candidate publicly assented to the faith into which he or she was being incorporated. In the Eucharist, the Church gave thanks according to prayers that presupposed creation, incarnation, redemption, resurrection, and the hope of the age to come (the *Didache* 9–10; Justin Martyr, *First Apology* [*Apologia I*] 65–67). In doxology, the Church named God as Father, Son, and Holy Spirit, thereby praising what she believed. Liturgy thus functioned as a living confession of faith—repeated, memorized, and received across generations, especially where written texts were few and literacy was rare.

As doctrinal disputes arose, the Church did not create new beliefs but rendered explicit the faith she had already confessed. The ancient symbols (*symbola*) and conciliar definitions gave stable and public form to what had long been believed, prayed, and taught. Their authority lay not in novelty, but in reception: they were read aloud, received into worship, taught to catechumens, and used as measures of communion. In them, the Church spoke together so that the same faith might be confessed with one voice across lands and tongues.

What follows therefore does not seek to exhaust the mystery of God, nor to impose speculative determinations beyond what the Church has universally received. It confines itself to those affirmations that have remained constant in the Church's confession: taught in catechesis, sealed in baptism, enacted in prayer, and guarded by the common judgment of the Church. It speaks where the Church has spoken together, and it remains silent where the Church has not bound the conscience.

The Articles that follow have been set forth through attentive regard to the Church's reception across time: to what has been confessed everywhere, always, and by all in substance; to what recurs across the Church's modes of remembrance—Scripture, confession, prayer, teaching, and judgment; and to what proves necessary for the coherence of the gospel's proclamation and the integrity of Christian worship. Each Article is framed according to the Church's customary manner of speech—belief, confession, teaching, praise— so that the form of words accords with the use by which the faith has been handed on.

Yet in every case, the Church's speech here is not descriptive only, but declarative and binding upon herself. To say "We believe" or "We confess" is to commit the Church publicly to what she has received, to stand within it, and to hand it on unchanged. The authority claimed is therefore ministerial and custodial: not the authority of origin, but of faithful stewardship; not mastery over the truth, but obedience to it. What follows is not offered as a rival to Holy Scripture, nor as a substitute for creed or council, but as a structured witness to the same faith they confess—ordered so that the Church may believe, confess, teach, pray, and give thanks in continuity with the saints who have gone before.

To the Father, through the Son, in the Holy Spirit, be glory, now and unto the ages of ages. Amen.

How This Statement Is Meant to Be Used

This Statement of Faith is intended for use within the life of the Church, not as a private instrument of belief, but as a common measure of confession, instruction, and prayerful remembrance. It is ordered toward formation rather than argument, unity rather than distinction, and reception rather than innovation.

Initiation into Faith (Catechetical Use).
This Statement may serve as a rule for teaching and learning, especially for those being prepared for baptism or for fuller participation in the life of the Church. Its Articles are arranged to reflect the shape of the apostolic proclamation, so that learners may be grounded first in what is confessed together before engaging matters that admit of further inquiry. In this use, the Statement guides faithful reading of Scripture without replacing it, and orients learning within the bounds of the received faith.

Public Worship (Liturgical Use).
This Statement may be employed in settings of communal prayer and public worship, particularly where the articulation of faith accompanies the proclamation of the Word. Its language is intentionally suited for public hearing and shared assent, echoing the rhythms of baptismal and creedal confession. In such use, the Articles are not explained but enacted, spoken together before God as acts of praise and trust.

Professional Standard (Ecclesial Use).
This Statement may also function as a public confession of faith for assemblies, institutions, or communities seeking to express continuity with the faith of the undivided Church. In such use, it serves not as a test of private conscience, but as a shared articulation of what is held in common. It defines the center without exhausting the whole, and binds only where the Church has long spoken together.

In all its uses, this Statement is to be received as a witness rather than a weapon, as a measure rather than a tool of exclusion, and as a means of clarity ordered toward peace. Where it is used rightly, it will not draw attention to itself, but will point beyond itself to the faith it serves, the Church that confesses it, and the God who is its true subject and end.

Contents

Reader's Preface ii

Authority Statement: Proemium & Ecclesial Voice v

How This Statement Is Meant to Be Used ix

Part I. The Statement of Faith 1

Article I. The One God 2

Article II. God the Creator 3

Article III. Christ, Son and Lord 4

Article IV. The Incarnation 5

Article V. Christ's Saving Death 6

Article VI. Resurrection and Exaltation 7

Article VII. The Holy Spirit 8

Article VIII. The One Holy Church 9

Article IX. Forgiveness of Sins 10

Article X. Future Coming & Judgment 11

Article XI. Life of the Age to Come 12

Statement of Faith (Concise Form) 13

Part II. Initiation into Faith 14

Catechetical Orientation: Doctrinal Instruction 15

Catechetical Reception—The One God 17

Catechetical Reception—God the Creator 20

Catechetical Reception—Christ, Son and Lord 24

Catechetical Reception—The Incarnation 28

Catechetical Reception—Christ's Saving Death 32

Catechetical Reception—Resurrection and Exaltation 36

Catechetical Reception—The Holy Spirit 40

Catechetical Reception—The One Holy Church 45

Catechetical Reception—Forgiveness of Sins 48

Catechetical Reception—Future Coming and Judgment 52

Catechetical Reception—Life of the Age to Come 55

Part III. Public Worship..**58**

    Liturgical Orientation: Doctrinal Enactment..59

    Gathering and Invocation 61

    Proclamation of the Word..64

    Corporate Confession of Faith...67

    Intercessory Prayer and Thanksgiving..70

    Eucharistic Thanksgiving..74

    Doxology and Sending..78

Part IV. Professional Standard **81**

    Communal Orientation: Doctrinal Statements 82

    Placement and Use Guidance 84

    Churches, Congregations, Communions 85

    Universities, Schools, Ministries, Charities..86

    Networks, Partnerships, Societies, Alliances..86

    Minimal Attestation of Reception..88

    On The Stability and Use of This Edition (Colophon)...........................89

    Rule of Faith (Delimiting the Confession) 90

    Doxology..91

PART I.
THE STATEMENT OF FAITH

(ARTICLES OF FAITH PROPER)

Article I.
The One God

De Deo Uno

We believe in one God, the LORD.

We confess that there is no other.

Article II.
God the Creator

De Deo Creatore

We believe that the one God is the Creator of heaven and earth, of all things visible and invisible.

Article III.
Christ, Son and Lord

De Christo Filio et Domino

We confess Jesus Christ, God's Son, as our Lord.

Article IV.
The Incarnation

De Incarnatione

We believe and confess that for us and for our salvation

the Son of God, the Word, became truly human.

We believe that he was conceived by the Holy Spirit and born of Mary.

Article V.
Christ's Saving Death

De Morte Salvifica Christi

We believe that Jesus Christ was crucified, died, and was buried.

We believe that he did this for our sins, according to the Scriptures.

Article VI.
Resurrection and Exaltation

De Resurrectione et Exaltatione

We believe that on the third day Jesus Christ rose bodily from the dead.

We believe that he appeared to witnesses.

We believe that he ascended into heaven and is seated at the right hand of the Father.

Article VII.
The Holy Spirit

De Spiritu Sancto

We believe in the Holy Spirit.

We believe that the Holy Spirit gives life.

We believe that the Holy Spirit unites the Church.

We believe that the Holy Spirit sanctifies the people of God.

Article VIII.
The One Holy Church

De Ecclesia Una Sancta

We acknowledge one, holy, catholic, and apostolic Church.

Article IX.
Forgiveness of Sins

De Remissione Peccatorum

We acknowledge the forgiveness of sins.

We acknowledge that God grants this forgiveness through Jesus Christ.

Article X.
Future Coming & Judgment

De Adventu Futuro et Iudicio

We believe that Jesus Christ will come again in glory to judge the living and
the dead.

We believe that his kingdom will have no end.

Article XI.
Life of the Age to Come

Vita Saeculi Venturi

We believe that God will raise the dead.

We believe in the resurrection of the body and the life of the age to come.

Statement of Faith
(Concise Form)

This statement is a summary of the Articles of Faith set forth in the full Statement of Faith and is intended for public and institutional reference.

We believe that the one God is the Creator of heaven and earth, of all things visible and invisible.

We confess Jesus Christ, God's Son, as our Lord.

We believe and confess that for us and for our salvation the Son of God, the Word, became truly human, conceived by the Holy Spirit, and born of Mary.

We believe that Jesus Christ was crucified, died, and was buried for our sins, according to the Scriptures.

We believe that on the third day Jesus Christ rose bodily from the dead, appeared to witnesses, ascended into heaven, and is seated at the right hand of the Father.

We believe in the Holy Spirit, who gives life, unites the Church, and sanctifies the people of God.

We acknowledge one, holy, catholic, and apostolic Church.

We acknowledge the forgiveness of sins, which God grants through Jesus Christ.

We believe that Jesus Christ will come again in glory to judge the living and the dead, and his kingdom will have no end.

We believe that God will raise the dead, granting the resurrection of the body and the life of the age to come.

PART II.
INITIATION INTO FAITH

(CATHECHISM)

Catechetical Orientation:
Doctrinal Instruction

The Articles of Faith set forth in this Statement are given for catechetical reception within the life of the Church. They are not offered as private theological reflections, nor as provisional summaries subject to individual revision, but as public ecclesial speech received, guarded, and handed on. In catechetical use, they function as a rule of teaching—a stable and shared point of reference by which the faith once delivered is learned, rehearsed, and spoken together, so that those who are instructed may be formed not only in understanding but in confession.

From the beginning, catechesis has served as the Church's ordered means of initiation into this common faith. In the earliest communities, instruction preceded baptism as a required ecclesial discipline, shaping belief, life, and readiness for sacramental incorporation. The *Teaching of the Twelve Apostles* (*Didache*) presupposes sustained moral and doctrinal formation before the baptismal rite, including instruction in the "Two Ways" and communal fasting (*Didache* 1–6; 7). Justin Martyr likewise describes catechumens as those who have been taught, who assent to the truth of what is taught, and who are then baptized and admitted to the Eucharistic assembly (Justin Martyr, *First Apology* [*Apologia I*] 61–67). The *Apostolic Tradition* attests a multi-year catechumenate marked by moral scrutiny, doctrinal instruction, and final examination before baptism (*Apostolic Tradition* 15–21). Catechesis thus functioned not as optional education but as the normative pathway into the Church's sacramental life.

This catechetical formation was simultaneously the primary vehicle for transmitting the rule of faith. Before the formal fixation of conciliar creeds, the Church taught a stable summary of apostolic doctrine through memorization, repetition, and confession. Irenaeus of Lyons describes this rule as universally held and taught across geographically dispersed churches, functioning as the measure by which Scripture is rightly confessed and novelty excluded (Irenaeus of Lyons, *Against Heresies* [*Adversus Haereses*] I.10.1–2; III.4.1). Tertullian treats this catechetical transmission as the criterion of orthodoxy over against heretical innovation (Tertullian, *On the Prescription of Heretics* [*De Praescriptione Haereticorum*] 13; 21). What would later be known as baptismal creeds, such as the Old Roman Symbol, emerged first within this catechetical context as spoken confessions placed on the lips of those entering the Church.

Catechesis also formed Christian life. Instruction concerned not only what was to be believed but how the baptized were to live. The ethical weight of the *Didache*, the moral urgency of Cyril of Jerusalem's *Pre-Catechetical Lecture* (*Procatechesis*), and Augustine's insistence that catechesis shape the affections and narrative self-understanding of converts all testify that catechesis aimed at habituation into a way of life consonant with the Church's confession (Cyril of Jerusalem, *Pre-Catechetical Lecture* [*Procatechesis*]; Augustine of Hippo, *On the Catechizing of the Uninstructed* [*De catechizandis rudibus*]). Belief and practice were formed together, without reduction of doctrine to moralism or of ethics to abstraction.

This formation was governed by a disciplined pedagogical economy. Certain mysteries, particularly those concerning the sacraments, were taught only after baptism. Cyril's *Mystagogical Catecheses* and Ambrose of Milan's *On the Mysteries* (*De Mysteriis*) presuppose a prior catechetical formation that orders when and how doctrine is disclosed, safeguarding reverence and integrity through deliberate sequencing. Catechesis was therefore regulated instruction, not open-ended discourse.

Throughout, catechesis culminated in corporate confession. The goal was not private mastery but the formation of ecclesial subjects capable of speaking the Church's faith as their own. Baptismal interrogations—"Do you believe…?"—functioned as catechetical summaries enacted liturgically, binding the catechumen to the Church's confession through first-person plural speech. To learn the faith was to learn to say *credimus* with the Church.

The catechetical materials that accompany each Article in this Statement are ordered according to this received pattern. Each Article is presented first as a fixed, memorizable confession spoken in the voice of the Church, not as a thesis to be argued toward but as a sentence to be learned, rehearsed, and owned. Instruction proceeds from confession, not toward it. What follows does not replace liturgical enactment, nor does it attempt to exhaust doctrine. Rather, it explains the faith already confessed by tracing its reception across the Church's diachronic memory-forms—Scripture, apostolic proclamation, patristic rule, baptismal practice, and conciliar stabilization—so that understanding may grow without displacing mystery, and clarity may be gained without narrowing the scope of faithful reflection.

Scripture is therefore read in communion with the Church's confession; historical witness is presented as testimony, not adjudication; and diversity of theological reflection is acknowledged without dissolving unity of belief. The aim of this catechesis is formation in the common faith of the Church, so that belief, understanding, worship, and life may grow together in continuity with what has been received, confessed, and handed on from the beginning.

Catechetical Reception—The One God

Function	Witness of the People of God by the Spirit	Instructor Cues
Proemial Orientation	You are not learning a private opinion, nor receiving a new speculation, but entering the confession the Church has guarded and handed on from the beginning, so that your mouth may speak with the people of God what God has made known and what the saints have taught in every place.	Remind catechumens: "received, not invented"; posture of listening and assent.
Doctrinal Proposition Asserted	We believe in one God, the LORD, and we confess that there is no other.	Have them repeat the sentence slowly, together, as memorization.
Diachronic Reception Anchoring	In the ancient confession of Israel the LORD first bound his people to himself by a spoken identity-word: "Hear, O Israel: the LORD our God, the LORD is one" (Deuteronomy 6:4), so that the people would not merely discuss God, but belong to him alone by a settled confession.	Note "confession as belonging"; connect to learning to say "we believe."
	And in the Church's fixed doxological praise, where the one God is named and glorified in common speech, the confession of the LORD's unique deity is carried forward as worship rather than argument, so that praise itself becomes a durable boundary against every rival claim to divine honor.	Emphasize daily rehearsal; monotheism as habituated speech.
	The same teaching was fixed with explicit exclusion, so that the confession would not weaken into mere preference: "The LORD is God… there is no other besides him" (Deuteronomy 4:35; cf. 4:39), establishing that the worship and trust due to the LORD cannot be divided without betraying the truth confessed.	Emphasize "no other" as boundary; distinguish from "greatest god" or "God is the greatest".
	Therefore the LORD gave a command that is also a confession in action, "You shall have no other gods before me" (Exodus 20:3), by which the people learned that to confess the one God is to refuse rival devotions in practice, and that the confession is meant to govern life as well as speech.	Ask for concrete examples of "rival devotions" in ancient setting (idols, household gods).

When the nations surrounded Israel and temptation multiplied, the prophets drove the confession into an irreversible clarity: "I am the LORD, and there is no other" (Isaiah 45:5; cf. 46:9), so that the Church, reading these words, would understand that the LORD's uniqueness is not a local custom but the truth of God himself, received and preserved in the people's public memory.	Stress prophetic "clarification under pressure"; connect to perseverance.
Our Lord Jesus Christ did not set this confession aside, but named it as first instruction, replying, "Hear, O Israel... the Lord is one" (Mark 12:29), showing that the catechumen's confession is not foreign to the Gospel but stands at its threshold as the Church's unbroken beginning.	Mark this as "first instruction"; have catechumens repeat Mark 12:29.
As the apostles preached among the Gentiles, where idols were many, they spoke the same faith with the same exclusion: "there is no God but one... for us there is one God, the Father" (1 Corinthians 8:4–6), so that the Church might confess the one LORD with settled clarity amid the nations, receiving this pattern as the Spirit-guided apostolic rule for speech and worship.	Explain Corinth context briefly; note "for us" = Church's communal confession.
For this reason the ancient teachers summarized the faith as a rule to be guarded against novelty, confessing, "There is one God Almighty... this is the God of Abraham and Isaac and Jacob, above whom there is no other God" (Irenaeus of Lyons, *Against Heresies* [*Adversus Haereses*] I.10.1), so that what was confessed in Israel and preached by the apostles would be preserved as the Church's stable measure in every place and time.	Identify Irenaeus as early bishop-teacher; highlight "above whom there is no other."
The same confession was set upon the lips of the baptized at the font, when the minister asked, "Do you believe in God, the Father Almighty?" and the one being baptized answered, "I believe" (*Apostolic Tradition* 21), so that the one God would be confessed not only in reading and teaching but in the very act of entrance into Christ's people.	Mimic the interrogatory rhythm aloud; connect confession to baptismal identity.

	And in the Church's fixed doxological praise, where the one God is named and glorified in common speech, the confession of the LORD's unique deity is carried forward as worship rather than argument, so that praise itself becomes a durable boundary against rival claims to divine honor.	Identify doxology as confession-in-worship.
	And when the Church gathered in council to speak with one voice, she compressed this faith into the public symbol, "We believe in one God, Father Almighty" (Nicene Creed, 325), so that the one LORD would be confessed everywhere with a fixed and common speech, received, guarded, and transmitted by the Church as the sure and non-optional beginning of her proclamation.	Note "public symbol"; explain "We believe" as corporate voice.
Illocutionary Clarification	When the Church speaks this Article, she is not offering a private theory but performing a confession and a boundary: she proclaims the LORD as the one true God, bears witness to his uniqueness, and renounces every rival claim to worship by the words "there is no other."	Name the speech-acts: confession, proclamation, renunciation; keep it calm and firm.
Interrogation (Question and Answer)	The instructor says, "Whom do you worship and trust as God?" The catechumen answers, "I worship and trust the LORD alone, the one God." The instructor says, "Do you confess any other as God with him?" The catechumen answers, "I confess that there is no other."	Drill twice; ensure exact wording matches the Article.
Boundary Clarification Clause (Negative Definition)	This confession does not mean that the LORD is merely first among many, nor that he is one god beside other gods, nor that he shares his glory with rivals; rather, as it is written, "I am the LORD, and there is no other" (Isaiah 45:5), and therefore every so-called god is denied divine worship by the Church's confession.	Correct "best god" misunderstanding; keep tone non-polemical, but definite.
Formational & Existential Implication	Therefore this faith orders your whole allegiance: you are taught to call upon one God with an undivided heart, to pray without duplicity, to refuse the fear of many powers, and to stand with the Church in one voice, since "one God and Father of all" (Ephesians 4:6) gathers his people into a single confession and a single hope.	Connect to prayer practice and courage; avoid moralism—keep it allegiance-framed.
Catechetical Acclamation	This is the faith of the Church: we believe in one God, the LORD, and we confess that there is no other. Amen.	Have the group answer: "Amen."

Catechetical Reception—God the Creator

Function	Witness of the People of God by the Spirit	Instructor Cues
Proemial Orientation	Beloved catechumen, you are now being addressed within the Church's act of instruction, not as one seeking private insight, but as one receiving what has been handed down, guarded, and proclaimed before you. What you are about to hear is not newly reasoned nor privately discovered, but confessed by the people of God across generations as the truth by which the Church knows God and worships him.	Establish posture of reception; remind learner this is handed-on teaching.
Doctrinal Proposition Asserted	We believe that the one God is the Creator of heaven and earth, of all things visible and invisible, and that nothing which exists stands outside His creative will.	Invite memorization; ensure exact phrasing is retained.
Diachronic Reception Anchoring	At the beginning of the sacred Scriptures, the people of God confess, "In the beginning God created the heavens and the earth" (Genesis 1:1), a proclamation received from Israel's earliest memory and continuously read in the assembly as the foundational declaration that all that is comes from the one God alone. This confession arose not as speculation but as Israel's worshipful acknowledgment of the LORD who brought forth the ordered world, and it fixed forever the Church's speech so that creation is attributed neither to fate nor to lesser powers, but to God Himself, a truth preserved and transmitted by the community under the faithful guidance of the Holy Spirit.	Recall Genesis as read publicly; stress continuity from Israel to Church.
	In the praise of Israel's worship, it is sung, "By the word of the LORD the heavens were made, and by the breath of his mouth all their host" (Psalm 33:6), a hymn arising from the monarchic and exilic periods and used liturgically to confess that both the visible heavens and their unseen hosts owe their existence to God. This doxological form stabilized the distinction between what is seen and unseen without division of authorship, preparing the Church to confess one Creator of the whole, a confession the Spirit confirmed by embedding it in the prayer of the people.	Note hymn as worship, not theory; highlight seen and unseen.

Through the prophets, the LORD declares, "I am the LORD, who made all things, who alone stretched out the heavens" (Isaiah 44:24), spoken in the exilic period to exclude all intermediaries and rivals. This proclamation sharpened the Church's later confession by fixing the Creator article as a boundary against divided origins, and it was received as authoritative speech by the same Spirit who gathers the Church into fidelity to the one Maker.	Emphasize exclusion of rivals; connect to boundary-setting.
In apostolic proclamation to the nations, the Church announces, "We bring you good news, that you should turn… to a living God who made the heaven and the earth and the sea and all that is in them" (Acts 14:15), a missionary confession spoken aloud in the first century as the Church distinguished the Creator from idols. This kerygmatic use fixed the doctrine of God the Creator as a non-negotiable element of the faith confessed before the world, received corporately and preserved by the Spirit through apostolic preaching.	Identify missionary context; stress public confession.
In the apostolic hymn received by the Church, it is proclaimed that "all things were created… visible and invisible" (Colossians 1:16), a first-century confession sung in worship that supplied the precise language later fixed in creeds. By uniting the visible and invisible realms under a single act of creation, this hymn irreversibly stabilized the Church's language, a stabilization confirmed by its enduring liturgical and communal reception under the Spirit's guidance.	Draw attention to exact wording; note hymn form.
When Justin confessed before the magistrates, he declared God to be the "Maker and Fashioner of the whole creation, visible and invisible" (*Acts of Justin*, interrogation summary, c. 165), a juridical confession made under threat of death. In this witness the Creator article was bound publicly to the whole scope of reality, and its confessional force was sealed in the Church's memory.	Note martyr context; stress costliness of confession.

	In the Rule of Faith handed on against false teaching, the Church confesses "one God... who made the heaven, the earth, the seas, and all things in them" (Irenaeus, Against Heresies I.10), articulated in the late second century for catechetical instruction. This formulation stabilized the Creator article as universal and indivisible, and its widespread reception shows the Spirit's work in guarding the Church's confession.	Indicate catechetical use; stress universality.
	In the great council of the Church, the bishops confessed, "We believe in one God... Maker of all things visible and invisible" (Nicene Creed, 325), a conciliar and liturgical definition arising to secure the faith of the whole Church. This act fixed the Creator doctrine in an ecumenical symbol, rendering it stable, repeatable, and binding, received by the Church as a faithful act of the Holy Spirit guiding her into truth.	Mark conciliar authority; note permanence.
	And as the Church's baptismal creed was received into universal liturgical use, she fixed the Creator confession in the compressed and repeatable form, "Maker of heaven and earth, of all that is seen and unseen" (Niceno-Constantinopolitan Creed, 381), thereby sealing the Creator article as a memorized, said, and prayed public form by which the faithful learned to name God as the sole origin of all reality.	Stress "compressed creed-form"; emphasize liturgical repetition and memorability.
	In the Church's eucharistic thanksgiving, God is habitually praised as the giver from whom all good gifts come, so that creation is confessed not only as origin but as the continuing ground of gratitude and worship, a pattern fixed by repeated communal performance rather than private speculation.	Connect Creator doctrine to thanksgiving and worship.
Illocutionary Clarification	When the Church says, "We believe," she is not offering an opinion but performing a confession that binds her speech, worship, and identity to the one God as Creator of all that is.	Clarify speech-act; emphasize performative nature.
Interrogation (Question and Answer)	The instructor asks, "Do you believe in God the Creator?" and the catechumen responds, "I believe in one God, the Creator of heaven and earth, of all things visible and invisible."	Use aloud; ensure call-and-response cadence.
Boundary Clarification Clause (Negative Definition)	This confession does not allow that the world arose by chance, nor that matter exists apart from God's will, nor that unseen powers share in the act of creation, for the Church confesses one Creator alone.	State exclusions calmly; avoid polemic.

Formational & Existential Implication	By confessing God as Creator of all that is, the catechumen learns to receive the world as gift, to worship the Maker rather than the made, and to live within a created order sustained by God's faithful sovereignty.	Connect belief to orientation of life and worship.
Catechetical Acclamation	This is the faith of the Church: we believe in one God, the Creator of all that is. Amen.	Invite communal assent.

Catechetical Reception—Christ, Son and Lord

Function	Witness of the People of God by the Spirit	Instructor Cues
Proemial Orientation	You are now being taught the confession which the Church herself speaks and hands on, not as a private opinion nor as a conclusion drawn by reasoning, but as the living faith received from the apostles and guarded in her worship, preaching, and sacraments. Attend, therefore, not as a spectator, but as one being formed to speak with the Church and to stand within her voice.	Establish posture of reception rather than inquiry.
Doctrinal Proposition Asserted	The Church confesses Jesus Christ, God's Son, as our Lord, acknowledging him as the one whom God has revealed, whom the Church names, and to whom the faithful belong in obedience and worship.	Require memorization of the proposition.
Diachronic Reception Anchoring	This confession is already heard in the apostolic proclamation, when those who encountered Jesus named him not merely as teacher but as Lord and Son, confessing with their mouths what the Church would never cease to say: "Jesus is Lord" (Romans 10:9) and acclaiming him with Thomas's words, "My Lord and my God" (John 20:28), uttered at the threshold of the resurrection faith at the end of the first century, where proclamation, worship, and confession converge and fix the language by which the Church names Jesus.	Emphasize scriptural confession as public speech.
	In the earliest hymnic and doxological material received within the New Testament itself, the Church addressed Jesus with the divine name and posture of worship, confessing that "at the name of Jesus every knee should bow ... and every tongue confess that Jesus Christ is Lord" (Philippians 2:9–11), a liturgical acclamation that identifies Jesus as the bearer of the LORD's name and situates his lordship within the worship owed to God alone.	Identify hymn as worship, not commentary.
	This confession was bound to the Church's initiatory life from an early period, as baptismal practice publicly required converts to confess Jesus as Son and Lord before entering the water, thereby showing that this was not optional speech but the decisive boundary by which one entered the Christian life (cf. Acts 8:36–38; and the early baptismal confession tradition associated with Acts 8:37).	Connect confession explicitly to baptism.

The primitive baptismal acclamation "Jesus is Lord," presupposed in apostolic teaching and echoed in early catechesis, functioned as the minimal yet decisive confession by which converts renounced other allegiances and entered the lordship of Christ, uniting faith, speech, and obedience in a single performative act (cf. 1 Corinthians 12:3).	Stress exclusivity of allegiance.
At the beginning of the second century, Ignatius of Antioch confessed Jesus Christ in Eucharistic and pastoral exhortation as "the Son of God" and "our Lord," speaking of "the flesh of Jesus Christ, the Son of God" and "one flesh of our Lord Jesus Christ" in letters written on the way to martyrdom (Ignatius of Antioch, *Letter to the Smyrnaeans* [*Epistula ad Smyrnaeos*] 1; *Letter to the Ephesians* [*Epistula ad Ephesios*] 20), thereby fixing this confession not as speculation but as the language of worship, unity, and costly fidelity.	Note martyrdom context and Eucharistic tone.
The Church received the apostolic confession that Jesus Christ "committed no sin" and was without deceit (1 Peter 2:22), preserving this truth as integral to his saving work and divine sonship. This confession was echoed in early teaching, where the sinlessness of Christ was treated not as moral achievement but as a consequence of his divine identity and true humanity, a norm implicitly assumed in the Church's worship, proclamation, and sacramental life and preserved as part of the rule of faith (cf. Irenaeus of Lyons, *Against Heresies* [*Adversus Haereses*] III).	Tie sinlessness to identity, not example.
In early eucharistic prayers and communal worship, Jesus was directly addressed and invoked as Lord, particularly in the Aramaic cry "Maranatha" ("Our Lord, come"), preserved in the Church's prayer (1 Corinthians 16:22), demonstrating that the confession of Jesus as Lord was not only spoken about him but spoken to him in expectation and hope.	Emphasize address *to* Christ in prayer.

	Toward the end of the second century, Irenaeus of Lyons articulated the Church's received rule of faith, proclaiming "one Christ Jesus, the Son of God" and confessing "Christ Jesus, our Lord" as the faith held by the Church "though dispersed throughout the whole world" (Irenaeus of Lyons, *Against Heresies* [*Adversus Haereses*] I.10.1), stabilizing the confession as a universal norm by which teaching was measured and catechesis ordered, and affirming that this confession was preserved by the Church through the Spirit's guidance rather than by local invention.	Stress universality of the rule of faith.
	In the baptismal interrogations preserved in the early third century, candidates were asked directly whether they believed in "Christ Jesus, the Son of God," responding aloud before immersion (*Apostolic Tradition* 21), a practice that fixed the confession of Jesus as Son and Lord as a performative pledge made at the threshold of life in Christ and guarded by the Church as a stable and repeatable act of faith.	Highlight spoken response and communal hearing.
	Early doxologies and benedictions consistently placed Jesus within the divine identity, naming him as Lord alongside the Father and the Spirit (e.g., "Grace to you and peace from God our Father and the Lord Jesus Christ"), embedding his lordship into the Church's habitual speech of blessing, thanksgiving, and praise.	Note habitual, non-polemical usage.
	This confession reached its fullest conciliar stabilization when the Church declared with one voice, "We believe in one Lord Jesus Christ, the Son of God" at Nicaea in 325 and reaffirmed it in the baptismal creed of Constantinople in 381, embedding the confession irreversibly into the Church's public worship and instruction, so that to name Jesus otherwise would no longer be recognized as the Church's own speech.	Indicate conciliar authority without polemic.
Illocutionary Clarification	When the Church says, "We confess Jesus Christ, God's Son, as our Lord," she performs an act of confession and allegiance, not merely describing a belief but publicly naming the one to whom she belongs, bears witness, and offers worship, binding herself to this Lord in speech that is itself an act of faith.	Explain confession as action, not description.
Interrogation (Question and Answer)	The instructor asks, "Whom do you confess?" and the catechumen answers, "I confess Jesus Christ, God's Son, as my Lord," echoing the Church's own words as a spoken participation in her faith.	Use aloud, with clear vocal repetition.

Boundary Clarification Clause (Negative Definition)	This confession does not mean that Jesus is merely one lord among many, nor that he is called Son only by honor or adoption, nor that his lordship is symbolic or partial, but it excludes all speech that would diminish his true sonship from God or divide allegiance away from him.	Guard against dilution without naming opponents.
Formational & Existential Implication	To confess Jesus Christ as God's Son and our Lord orders the catechumen's understanding of belonging, so that life, prayer, and obedience are oriented toward him as the one whom the Church names above all others and under whose lordship the faithful now stand.	Connect confession to allegiance, not ethics.
Catechetical Acclamation	This is the faith of the Church; this is the confession we receive and speak together. Amen.	Invite communal assent.

Catechetical Reception—The Incarnation

Function	Witness of the People of God by the Spirit	Instructor Cues
Proemial Orientation	You are now being instructed in the faith that the Church has received and handed on concerning the mystery by which God has acted for our salvation, not as a matter of private insight or speculative teaching, but as a confession preserved in Scripture, proclaimed in worship, guarded in doctrine, and entrusted to those preparing to enter the life of Christ.	Establish attentive posture; remind catechumen of received authority.
Doctrinal Proposition Asserted	We believe and confess that for us and for our salvation the Son of God, the eternal Word, truly became human, conceived by the Holy Spirit and born of Mary.	Invite slow repetition; emphasize memorability.
Diachronic Reception Anchoring	The Church's confession begins in the apostolic proclamation that "the Word became flesh and dwelt among us" (John 1:14), spoken in the late first century as part of the Gospel's public proclamation, fixing forever that the eternal Word did not merely appear human but entered the fullness of embodied life, thereby grounding all later confession of the Incarnation in canonical testimony received and proclaimed by the Church under the guidance of the Holy Spirit.	Identify scriptural root; note public proclamation.
	From the beginning, Scripture named humanity as God's own image-bearing creature—"Let us make man in our image… So God created man in his own image" (Genesis 1:26–27)—so that when the Church confessed that "the Word became flesh" (John 1:14), she received the Incarnation as the Son's true assumption of the same human nature marked by divine-referential dignity, thereby anchoring the confession that Christ's humanity is neither illusory nor alien but the image-bearing flesh God created and now takes up for our salvation.	Emphasize: assumption of real humanity.
	The same apostolic witness declared that "God sent forth his Son, born of a woman" (Galatians 4:4), situating the Incarnation within salvation history and emphasizing real birth in time, a formulation arising within early catechetical preaching to stabilize the Church's confession against any denial of Christ's genuine humanity, and received as normative apostolic teaching.	Stress historical birth; connect to salvation.

Early Christian confession condensed this faith in brief formulas such as "God was manifested in the flesh" (1 Timothy 3:16), likely used in liturgical or catechetical contexts at the turn of the first and second centuries, crystallizing a concise and repeatable form that secured the Church's shared memory of the Incarnation across worship and instruction.

Note confessional brevity.

Against denials of Christ's true humanity, Ignatius of Antioch testified that Jesus Christ was "both of Mary and of God" and "truly born of a virgin," writing around 105 in letters received and circulated among the churches (Ignatius of Antioch, *Letter to the Smyrnaeans* [*Epistula ad Smyrnaeos*] 1–2), thereby binding divine identity and human birth together in a confession preserved by communal reception and episcopal teaching.

Highlight anti-docetic clarity.

By the late second century, the Church summarized its received faith by confessing "one Christ Jesus… who became incarnate for our salvation… and the birth from a virgin" (Irenaeus of Lyons, *Against Heresies* [*Adversus Haereses*] I.10.1), articulating the Incarnation within the rule of faith used for catechesis and doctrinal testing, thereby irreversibly linking incarnation, salvation, and virginal birth in the Church's normative memory.

Connect rule of faith to catechesis.

The Church confessed the Son's divine origin not as a temporal beginning but as an eternal relation, teaching that the Son is "begotten of the Father before all ages," language drawn from the Church's received reading of Scripture (cf. Psalm 2:7; John 1:18) and articulated against subordinationist distortions by confessing that the Son's generation belongs to God's own eternal life. This confession was received and stabilized when the bishops declared the Son to be "begotten from the Father, that is, from the substance of the Father" (Council of Nicaea, Creed, 325), fixing eternal generation as a normative boundary for confessing Christ's divine identity within the Church's common faith.

Emphasize "relation, not origin in time"; distinguish begetting from creation.

	This confession was fixed with decisive authority when the Church proclaimed that the Son was "incarnate from the Holy Spirit and the Virgin Mary" (Niceno-Constantinopolitan Creed, 381). It was further defended at Ephesus in 431 by affirming that the one born of Mary is truly the Word of God, thereby stabilizing the Church's language as a matter of shared faith, guarded in the Church's public confession guarded by the Holy Spirit.	Mark conciliar settlement.
	In confessing the Incarnation, the Church learned to speak of one and the same Christ acting in both divine and human ways, refusing any division of subject. This unity was clarified when Cyril of Alexandria insisted that "there is one Son, one Lord, Jesus Christ," teaching that the Word begotten of the Father is the same one born of Mary, so that the actions of both natures belong to one person (Cyril of Alexandria, *Third Letter to Nestorius* [*Epistula III ad Nestorium*], read, examined, and received as consistent with Nicene faith at the Council of Ephesus, 431). Thus the Church's confession was anchored against any account of the Incarnation as a conjunction of persons rather than a true personal union.	Stress "one acting subject"; avoid technical speculation.
	As disputes arose concerning whether Christ's humanity or divinity was diminished or confused, the Church confessed with precision that the one Lord Jesus Christ is "acknowledged in two natures, without confusion, without change, without division, without separation," preserving the fullness of both divinity and humanity (Council of Chalcedon, 451). This formula did not introduce a new faith but safeguarded the Church's inherited confession, stabilizing the Incarnation normatively so that Christ could be confessed as truly God and truly man without reduction or mixture.	Emphasize protection, not innovation; "guardrails, not theory."
Illocutionary Clarification	When the Church says these words, she does not merely describe a past event but confesses, proclaims, and bears witness to God's saving act, binding herself to the truth that the eternal Son has entered human history for the redemption of the world.	Name the speech-act.

Interrogation (Question and Answer)	The instructor asks, "Why do we confess that the Son of God became truly human?" and the catechumen answers, "Because for us and for our salvation the Word was conceived by the Holy Spirit and born of Mary."	Practice oral exchange.
Boundary Clarification Clause (Negative Definition)	This confession does not mean that the Son merely appeared human, nor that his humanity was incomplete or illusory, nor that his birth was separate from his divine identity, but that the one eternal Word truly assumed human flesh in a real birth from Mary.	Guard against misunderstanding.
Formational & Existential Implication	By confessing the Incarnation, you are formed to recognize that God has drawn near in human life itself, sanctifying human flesh and history, and calling you to live in allegiance to Christ who shares fully in what it means to be human.	Relate belief to identity.
Catechetical Acclamation	This is the faith of the Church, received from the apostles, confessed through the ages, and handed on for our salvation. Amen.	Lead communal assent.

Catechetical Reception—Christ's Saving Death

Function	Witness of the People of God by the Spirit	Instructor Cues
Proemial Orientation	Beloved hearer of the Church's teaching, you are now instructed in the mystery of the saving death of Jesus Christ as it has been received, confessed, and handed on within the Church from the beginning, not as a private opinion nor as a newly reasoned account, but as a truth entrusted to the saints and proclaimed in word, sacrament, and confession for the life of the world.	Invite attentive silence and recollection of the Passion narrative.
Doctrinal Proposition Asserted	We believe that Jesus Christ was crucified, died, and was buried for our sins according to the Scriptures, and that this saving death was accomplished once for all in obedience to the Father and for the redemption of humankind.	Have catechumens repeat the sentence aloud together.
Diachronic Reception Anchoring	The Church first received and confessed this faith in the apostolic proclamation itself, when Paul delivered what he himself had received, declaring, "that Christ died for our sins according to the Scriptures, and that he was buried" (1 Corinthians 15:3–4), a formulation transmitted in the mid-first century as a sacred summary of the Gospel preached in the assemblies, which fixed the death-for-sins and burial of Christ as non-negotiable content of the apostolic tradition and was preserved by the Church as authoritative teaching under the guidance of the Holy Spirit.	Emphasize "received" and "handed on" as technical terms.
	This saving death was already confessed by the Church as "according to the Scriptures," meaning not only that the events occurred, but that they were understood through Israel's prophetic and typological witness, so that Christ's death was received as the fulfillment of God's saving purpose foretold and now accomplished, a rule of interpretation embedded in apostolic proclamation itself.	Stress "according to the Scriptures" as interpretive rule, not proof-texting.

This same confession was bound to the Church's sacramental life when the apostle taught, "as often as you eat this bread and drink the cup, you proclaim the Lord's death until he comes" (1 Corinthians 11:26), situating the saving death of Christ at the heart of Eucharistic worship in the first century, so that the Church's repeated liturgical action irreversibly joined belief in the death of Christ to its continual proclamation, a pattern sustained by communal reception rather than individual interpretation.

Point to the altar as the place of proclamation.

The dominical words spoken over the cup— "poured out for many for the forgiveness of sins" (Matthew 26:28)—were received and repeated by the Church as fixed liturgical speech, so that the meaning of Christ's death as redemptive and sin-remitting was not only taught but enacted and proclaimed each time the Eucharist was celebrated, stabilizing the saving significance of the cross as a living memory-form.

Emphasize repetition of the Lord's own words in worship.

In the late second century, Irenaeus of Lyons articulated the rule of truth received in the churches, including Christ's passion as part of the apostolic faith proclaimed everywhere and always, affirming that the Church confesses "the passion" of Christ as taught by the apostles (Irenaeus of Lyons, *Against Heresies* [*Adversus Haereses*] I.10.1), thereby stabilizing the saving death within a normative summary used to guard the faith against distortion and to transmit it intact under the Church's discernment in the Holy Spirit.

Note the use of this summary for instruction before baptism.

This confession was further fixed in baptismal symbols of the Roman Church, which professed that Christ "under Pontius Pilate was crucified and buried," a formula in use from the second to fourth centuries as candidates entered the waters of rebirth, binding personal initiation to the historical and saving death of Christ and confirming this belief as an identity-marking confession sustained by ecclesial practice.

Recall the baptismal interrogation context.

	The universal Church solemnly stabilized this confession in the fourth century through the ecumenical creed, proclaiming that Christ "was crucified for us under Pontius Pilate; he suffered and was buried" (Niceno-Constantinopolitan Creed, 381), establishing an authoritative and worshiped confession that fixed the passion, death, and burial of Christ as a definitive and universally binding expression of the faith received and preserved by the Church in the Holy Spirit.	Indicate creedal recitation in the liturgy.
	Patristic teaching deepened the Church's understanding of the saving efficacy of this death when Justin Martyr testified that "Christ has redeemed us by being crucified on the tree" (Justin Martyr, *Dialogue with Trypho* [*Dialogus cum Tryphone*] 95), written around the middle of the second century in a context of instruction and defense, clarifying that the crucifixion was not merely narrated but confessed as redemptive "for us," a meaning received and retained within the Church's common teaching.	Stress "for us" as soteriological language.
	The Church's liturgy gave enduring voice to this faith as eucharistic prayers and chants reiterated the cup as the blood "shed for the remission of sins," so that the saving death was confessed not only in teaching but continually in worship. In this repeated doxological form, the Church carried the meaning of the Cross forward as living memory and public proclamation rather than private interpretation.	Invite recollection of eucharistic words.
Illocutionary Clarification	When the Church declares that Christ was crucified, died, and was buried for our sins, she performs an act of confession and proclamation, bearing authoritative witness to God's saving deed and binding herself to this truth in her worship, teaching, and communal life.	Clarify that this is a confession, not a theory.
Interrogation (Question and Answer)	The instructor asks, "What do you confess concerning Jesus Christ?" and the catechumen answers, "I confess that Jesus Christ was crucified, died, and was buried for my sins according to the Scriptures."	Practice the exchange aloud.

Boundary Clarification Clause (Negative Definition)	This confession does not mean that Christ only appeared to suffer, nor that his death was accidental or merely exemplary, nor that forgiveness comes apart from his obedient death and burial, for the Church confesses a real, saving death accomplished in history and received in faith.	Guard against docetic misunderstandings.
Formational & Existential Implication	By confessing the saving death of Christ, the catechumen is formed to understand salvation as a gift accomplished by God's act in Christ, to live under the sign of the Cross, and to belong to a people whose hope and worship are grounded in the Lord who gave himself for our sins.	Invite reverent reflection rather than moral exhortation.
Catechetical Acclamation	This is the faith of the Church; this is the faith handed down through the ages; we confess it together, and we say, Amen.	Lead the communal acclamation.

Catechetical Reception—Resurrection and Exaltation

Function	Witness of the People of God by the Spirit	Instructor Cues
Proemial Orientation	Beloved hearer of the faith, you are now instructed in what the Church has received and handed on concerning the victory of Jesus Christ over death and his exaltation in glory, not as a private account or symbolic reflection, but as the living confession proclaimed in the assembly and entrusted to those preparing to enter the saving mystery through baptism.	Address the catechumen directly and situate the teaching as received tradition.
Doctrinal Proposition Asserted	We believe that on the third day Jesus Christ rose bodily from the dead, that he appeared to chosen witnesses, that he ascended into heaven, and that he is seated at the right hand of the Father in glory.	Invite careful listening to a fixed and memorizable confession.
Diachronic Reception Anchoring	The Church first received this confession in the apostolic proclamation itself, when the blessed Apostle Paul handed on what he had received, declaring that "Christ died for our sins in accordance with the Scriptures, that he was buried, that he was raised on the third day in accordance with the Scriptures, and that he appeared" to many witnesses (1 Corinthians 15:3–8), a formula already in use by the middle of the first century to define the very content of the gospel and to bind the resurrection, the third day, and the appearances together as a single, non-negotiable proclamation guarded by the apostolic community under the guidance of the Holy Spirit.	Emphasize apostolic reception and transmission.
	The apostolic witness received the resurrection not as an isolated marvel but as the vindication of the crucified Lord, so that the Cross became the definitive measure of love itself: "By this we know love, that he laid down his life for us—and we ought to lay down our lives for the brothers" (1 John 3:16). Thus the Church learned to confess the Crucifixion as both the source of forgiveness and the pattern of the forgiven life, now lived under the lordship of the risen Christ.	Frame neighbor-love as participation in cruciform life, not optional virtue.

In the earliest catechetical manuals, the Church instructed converts in "the way of life and the way of death" (*Didache* 1–6), where love of neighbor, refusal of violence, generosity, and reconciliation functioned as concrete tests of whether one had truly received the saving work of Christ. In this pre-baptismal formation, moral responsibility was taught not as law apart from grace, but as the shape of the new life that follows from forgiveness and is sustained in hope of the risen Lord.

Keep the contrast sharp: *life* vs *death*, not "better vs worse." Tie explicitly to baptismal formation (this is *pre*-Eucharistic catechesis).

This proclamation was immediately joined to the confession of Christ's exaltation, as the apostolic preaching bore witness that God "raised him up" and exalted him "at his right hand," making him both Lord and Christ (Acts 2:24, 33, 36), a first-century kerygmatic articulation that fixed the resurrection not merely as return to life but as enthronement, thereby uniting Easter, Ascension, and session in the Church's earliest preaching as one coherent saving act received and proclaimed by the whole community.

Connect resurrection to exaltation and lordship.

Against those who denied the reality of Christ's risen flesh, the holy martyr Ignatius of Antioch testified that after the resurrection the Lord said, "Take, handle me, and see that I am not a bodiless demon," and that he ate and drank with his disciples, writing around the beginning of the second century (Ignatius of Antioch, *Letter to the Smyrnaeans* [*Epistula ad Smyrnaeos*] 3), thereby stabilizing the Church's confession that the resurrection was bodily and continuous with the crucified Jesus, a clarification preserved and received by the churches as a faithful guard against distortion of the apostolic witness.

Stress the bodily reality of the resurrection.

The Church confessed that Christ's resurrection was not a return to mortal life but an entrance into glorified, incorruptible existence, as the apostle proclaimed that Christ is "the firstfruits of those who have fallen asleep" and that the risen body is raised in power and glory (1 Corinthians 15:20, 42–44). This understanding was normatively received and preserved as the Church taught that the risen Christ inaugurates the transformed life of the age to come, guarding the resurrection against reduction to mere revivification or symbolic survival.

Stress "new mode of life," not resuscitation.

	In the baptismal confession of the Church of Rome, the resurrection and ascension were compressed into a fixed initiatory formula, confessing that Christ "rose again on the third day" and "ascended into heaven," as witnessed in the Old Roman Symbol used in mid-second-century baptismal catechesis, by which the Church bound new believers to this sequence as a performative act of entry into the faith, received and preserved as a rule of belief under the Spirit's care.	Note baptismal and initiatory use.
	This confession was further rehearsed and fixed in the Church's Paschal proclamation, where the resurrection on the third day was not merely recalled but celebrated corporately as the decisive victory of Christ over death, embedding Easter confession as a repeated, communal memory-form that shaped the Church's worship and expectation year after year.	Emphasize annual, corporate rehearsal; resurrection as acclamation.
	This confession reached full ecumenical stability when the Church, gathered in council, proclaimed that Christ "rose again on the third day according to the Scriptures, ascended into heaven, and is seated at the right hand of the Father" (Niceno-Constantinopolitan Creed, 381), thereby juridically and liturgically fixing the resurrection, ascension, and session as universally binding doctrine, received across the churches as the faithful articulation of the apostolic faith guarded by the Holy Spirit.	Highlight conciliar and universal reception.
	And as the Church prayed and praised the risen Christ as the one enthroned at the Father's right hand, the language of session and reign became a stable doxological grammar, so that exaltation was confessed not as metaphor but as present lordship receiving worship and shaping the Church's address to Christ in hope and confidence.	Connect enthronement to worship and prayer.
Illocutionary Clarification	When the Church speaks this Article, she does not recount a past event as history alone, but bears witness, confesses, and proclaims the living lordship of the risen and exalted Christ, performing an act of ecclesial confession that binds the speaker to the truth confessed.	Identify the act as confession and proclamation.

Interrogation (Question and Answer)	The instructor asks: Do you believe that Jesus Christ rose from the dead on the third day and now reigns in glory? The catechumen responds: I believe that he rose bodily from the dead, appeared to witnesses, ascended into heaven, and is seated at the right hand of the Father.	Use call-and-response aloud.
Boundary Clarification Clause (Negative Definition)	This confession does not mean that Christ merely survived in memory, spirit, or vision, nor that his exaltation is a metaphor or symbol only, but that the same Jesus who was crucified and buried truly rose in the body and was taken into heavenly glory, beyond corruption and death.	Clarify calmly what is excluded.
Formational & Existential Implication	By confessing the resurrection and exaltation of Christ, the catechumen is formed to recognize Jesus as the living Lord who reigns now, to worship him with the Church in hope and confidence, and to await the fulfillment of God's purposes under his sovereign rule.	Connect belief to worship and orientation of life.
Catechetical Acclamation	This is the faith of the Church, this is the faith handed down from the apostles, this is the faith in which we stand; Amen.	Lead the assembly in communal assent.

Catechetical Reception—The Holy Spirit

Function	Witness of the People of God by the Spirit	Instructor Cues
Proemial Orientation	Beloved catechumen, attend now to the faith which the Church herself has received, guarded, and handed on, not as a private insight nor as a new teaching, but as the living confession spoken by the people of God in every place and time, into which you are being instructed so that you may speak it with the Church and be formed by what you confess.	Establish posture of reception rather than inquiry. Emphasize ecclesial voice.
Doctrinal Proposition Asserted	We believe in the Holy Spirit, who gives life, who unites the Church into one body, and who sanctifies the people of God.	Invite memorization. Speak slowly and clearly.
Diachronic Reception Anchoring	From the beginning, the Church received the Holy Spirit as constitutive of Christian life and incorporation, as the Lord commanded that those who enter the Church be baptized "in the name of the Father and of the Son and of the Holy Spirit" (*Didache* 7.1), a late first- or early second-century baptismal instruction arising within catechumenal practice, by which the Spirit was irrevocably fixed as a necessary agent of initiation, so that Christian life, unity, and belonging were never conceived apart from the Spirit's named presence, a practice the Church received and preserved as normative under the Spirit's own guidance.	Note baptism as the primary context. Connect Spirit to initiation.
	This baptismal formula itself presupposes and enacts the Spirit's personal identity, naming the Holy Spirit alongside the Father and the Son within a single divine "name," thereby fixing the Spirit not as an impersonal power but as a distinct, co-named participant in the Church's entry into divine life.	Emphasize triadic naming as identity-bearing.
	In the Church's earliest Eucharistic prayer, the gathered community implored God that, as scattered bread is gathered into one, so the Church might be gathered into the kingdom (*Didache* 9.4), a late first- or early second-century liturgical thanksgiving that arose from communal worship and fixed the understanding that ecclesial unity is God's own work enacted in the assembly, thereby embedding the Spirit's unitive action into the Church's regular prayer and confirming this reception through repeated communal performance.	Highlight Eucharistic gathering. Stress unity as enacted, not abstract.

At Pentecost, the Church received the Holy Spirit as the divine agent who speaks, sends, and constitutes the apostolic community (Acts 2), a canonical narrative proclaimed publicly in worship and catechesis, by which the Spirit is identified as the one who proceeds from God, empowers witness, and inaugurates the Church's mission, thereby fixing the Spirit's personal agency at the Church's visible beginning.	Stress public proclamation and corporate reception.
In apostolic benediction, the Church was blessed in triadic form—"the grace of the Lord Jesus Christ, the love of God, and the fellowship of the Holy Spirit" (2 Corinthians 13:13)—a liturgical farewell that places the Spirit as the personal giver of communion alongside the Father and the Son, embedding Trinitarian identity into the Church's habitual speech of blessing.	Identify benediction as liturgical speech.
As baptismal confession took stable form, the Church learned to confess succinctly "and in the Holy Spirit, the holy Church" (Old Roman Symbol, 2nd–4th c.), a creed used in catechetical and baptismal contexts that bound the confession of the Spirit directly to the Church's identity, thereby stabilizing the doctrine that the Church's unity and holiness are not achievements but given realities grounded in the Spirit's presence, faithfully transmitted across generations.	Show creed as memory-form. Emphasize pairing of Spirit and Church.
In the baptismal interrogations preserved in the early third century, candidates were asked directly, "Do you believe in the holy Spirit and the holy Church and the resurrection of the flesh?" and answered aloud, "I believe," before being baptized (*Apostolic Tradition* 21), thereby fixing the Spirit as a distinct and necessary object of confession at the threshold of Christian initiation, heard and ratified by the gathered Church as a stable and repeatable act of faith.	Highlight spoken response and communal hearing; connect to the third baptismal immersion.

The Church confessed the Holy Spirit not only as active and life-giving, but as eternally related to God's inner life, receiving Jesus' own teaching that the Spirit "proceeds from the Father" (John 15:26). This confession was normatively fixed when the bishops declared the Spirit to be "the Lord and Giver of life, who proceeds from the Father" (Niceno-Constantinopolitan Creed, 381), establishing procession as a doctrinal boundary for catholic pneumatology, while leaving its precise articulation to later theological reflection.

Distinguish eternal relation from temporal mission. Discuss the filioque controversy.

In early doxological formulas, the Church glorified Father, Son, and Holy Spirit together—"Glory be to the Father, and to the Son, and to the Holy Spirit"—a fixed form of praise received across East and West, which identified the Spirit as a proper recipient of the same worship offered to the Father and the Son, thereby excluding any lesser or instrumental account of the Spirit.

Stress worship as doctrinally decisive.

This confession reached its most definitive pre-Schism articulation when the Church confessed the Holy Spirit as "the Lord and Giver of life… who is worshiped and glorified… who spoke by the prophets" (Niceno-Constantinopolitan Creed, 381), a conciliar definition arising from ecclesial clarification and universal reception, which irreversibly fixed the Spirit's identity as life-giving, divine, and sanctifying, embedding this confession permanently in liturgy and catechesis as received and guarded by the whole Church.

Mark conciliar authority. Stress irreversibility of this form.

By confessing the Spirit as "Lord" (κύριος) and naming him as the proper subject of worship and glory, the Church publicly aligned the Spirit with the divine identity confessed of the Father and the Son, not by speculative reasoning but by authoritative confession received and enacted in common prayer.

Note lordship language explicitly.

	The Church's teachers further received this confession in sacramental exposition, as Basil of Caesarea taught that "the Spirit imparts life" to those passing through the waters of baptism into resurrectional existence (Basil of Caesarea, *On the Holy Spirit* [*De Spiritu Sancto*] 15.35), a fourth-century catechetical and doctrinal context that clarified how the Spirit gives life concretely by sanctifying persons into a holy people, a teaching received as consonant with the Church's baptismal practice.	Connect doctrine to sacramental life.
	In the Church's ancient baptismal prayers, the minister implored God to sanctify the waters "by the Holy Spirit" so that those baptized might die and rise into life, a ritual form widely received in the Church's mature baptismal practice. Thus sanctification was fixed as an enacted petition rather than a metaphor, stabilizing the confession that holiness is conferred corporately by the Spirit's consecrating action.	Emphasize prayer as performative.
	Likewise, in the Eucharistic anaphora attributed to James, the Church repeatedly prayed that God would sanctify both the gifts and the people "by the presence of Thy all-holy Spirit" (*Liturgy of St. James* [Ἡ Θεία Λειτουργία τοῦ Ἁγίου Ἰακώβου], pre-Schism Eastern reception), a liturgical setting that permanently bound the Spirit's work to the sanctification of the people of God through worship, received and preserved by the Church in faithful continuity.	Stress repetition and communal reception.
Illocutionary Clarification	When the Church says, "We believe in the Holy Spirit," she is not describing a theory nor recalling a story, but confessing and proclaiming a living reality, publicly committing herself to the Spirit's life-giving, unifying, and sanctifying work as the ground of her existence and worship.	Name the act as confession and proclamation.
Interrogation (Question and Answer)	The instructor asks, "Do you believe in the Holy Spirit?" Catechumen responds, "I believe in the Holy Spirit, who gives life, who unites the Church, and who sanctifies the people of God."	Use oral rehearsal. Maintain exact wording.
Boundary Clarification Clause (Negative Definition)	This confession does not mean that life, unity, or holiness arise from human effort, natural vitality, or private inspiration, nor that the Spirit acts apart from the Church's baptism, worship, and confession, but excludes every notion that the Church creates herself or sanctifies herself by her own power.	Clarify without naming opponents.

Formational & Existential Implication	By confessing the Holy Spirit, the catechumen is formed to recognize that Christian life is received, that belonging to the Church is a gift of unity, and that holiness is God's consecrating work, so that one's life is oriented toward grateful participation rather than self-assertion.	Connect belief to orientation of life.
Catechetical Acclamation	This is the faith of the Church. Amen.	Invite communal assent.

Catechetical Reception—The One Holy Church

Function	Witness of the People of God by the Spirit	Instructor Cues
Proemial Orientation	You are now instructed in what the Church herself confesses about her own being, not as an idea formed by reflection, but as a reality received, lived, and named within the worship, discipline, and memory of the people of God. What you hear is not an individual opinion about community, but the Church's own acknowledgment of what she has been given to be in Christ and through the apostles.	Remind the catechumen that this teaching concerns the Church they are entering, not an abstract concept.
Doctrinal Proposition Asserted	We acknowledge one, holy, catholic, and apostolic Church, called together by God, founded upon the apostles, sanctified by Christ, and gathered into unity by the Holy Spirit.	Invite careful listening, as this sentence is to be learned and confessed.
Diachronic Reception Anchoring	The apostolic writings already confess the Church as one body grounded in divine unity, when the Apostle proclaims, "There is one body and one Spirit... one Lord, one faith, one baptism" (Ephesians 4:4–5), written in the latter half of the first century to heal divisions within the baptized community, thereby fixing unity not as a moral aspiration but as a given reality rooted in God's own oneness and received by the Church as normative.	Note the apostolic origin of the Church's unity.
	And because the Church is not self-assembled but made, the one body is enacted at the font, where "one baptism" incorporates the many into one communion, so that ecclesial unity is confessed and performed as an initiatory reality rather than a future ideal (cf. Ephesians 4:5; *Apostolic Tradition* 21).	Unity as "enacted incorporation," not mere ethics.
	The same apostolic witness anchors the Church's apostolic character when believers are told that they are "built upon the foundation of the apostles and prophets, Christ Jesus himself being the cornerstone" (Ephesians 2:20), a confession arising from the earliest missionary expansion of the Church and stabilizing apostolicity as visible continuity of teaching and life rather than mere historical memory, a reception guarded and transmitted in communal faith under the Spirit's guidance.	Emphasize continuity, not innovation.

At the beginning of the second century, Ignatius of Antioch names the Church "catholic" when he writes, "Wherever Jesus Christ is, there is the catholic Church" (Ignatius of Antioch, *Letter to the Smyrnaeans* [*Epistula ad Smyrnaeos*] 8.2), spoken to safeguard unity around the Eucharistic gathering and its ordered ministry, thereby crystallizing catholicity as communion with Christ present among the assembled faithful, a seed faithfully preserved in later confessions.	Draw attention to Eucharistic gathering.
In eucharistic gathering, the Church's oneness is repeatedly enacted as communion in one bread and one cup, so that catholic unity is not merely geographic but sacramental and visible, rehearsed as a stable communal form (cf. 1 Corinthians 10:16–17; *Didache* 9–10).	Stress "visible unity in worship."
In the later second century, Irenaeus of Lyons confesses the Church as one and universal when he teaches that "the Church, although dispersed throughout the whole world, has received from the apostles and their disciples this faith" (Irenaeus of Lyons, *Against Heresies* [*Adversus Haereses*] I.10.1), articulated against Gnostic fragmentation to stabilize the Church as geographically extended yet doctrinally singular, a rule received, guarded, and handed on by the whole Church under the Spirit's care.	Connect unity with shared faith.
In the mid-third century, Cyprian of Carthage confesses the Church's unity by proclaiming, "The Church is one, though she is spread abroad far and wide into a multitude by an increase of fruitfulness" (Cyprian of Carthage, *On the Unity of the Church* [*De unitate ecclesiae*] 5), spoken amid schism to fix permanently the confession that multiplication does not divide the Church's oneness, a reception embedded in discipline and worship as Spirit-guided preservation of ecclesial identity.	Note unity amid diversity.
In catechetical instruction at Jerusalem, Cyril teaches candidates that the Church "is called catholic because it extends throughout the whole world, and because it teaches universally and completely all the doctrines" (Cyril of Jerusalem, *Catechetical Lectures* [*Catecheses*] 18.23), a mid-fourth-century exposition given to baptismal candidates that deepened the meaning of "catholic" without altering it, ensuring its stable reception within catechesis and liturgy alike.	Clarify meaning of "catholic."

	This reception reaches definitive conciliar form when the Church confesses in the Niceno-Constantinopolitan Creed, "We believe in one, holy, catholic, and apostolic Church" (381), a formulation arising to safeguard the integrity of faith and communion across the whole Church, permanently fixing these four notes as non-optional marks of ecclesial identity, received, prayed, and transmitted by the Church as guided by the Holy Spirit.	Identify this as the Church's fixed confession.
Illocutionary Clarification	When the Church says, "We acknowledge one, holy, catholic, and apostolic Church," she performs an act of communal recognition and allegiance, naming the body into which believers are incorporated and binding herself to this received reality as the sphere of faith, worship, and apostolic continuity.	Explain that this is a public act of acknowledgment.
Interrogation (Question and Answer)	The instructor asks: "What do you acknowledge concerning the Church?" The catechumen answers: "I acknowledge one, holy, catholic, and apostolic Church."	Practice the exchange aloud if appropriate.
Boundary Clarification Clause (Negative Definition)	This acknowledgment does not confess many churches divided in essence, nor a merely human association formed by choice, nor a hidden fellowship detached from teaching and sacrament, but the one visible and confessed Church founded by Christ and sustained through apostolic faith and communion.	Guard against misunderstanding.
Formational & Existential Implication	By acknowledging the Church, you are oriented not toward isolation but toward belonging, receiving faith, life, and sanctification within a communion that precedes you and will endure beyond you, shaping how you worship God and recognize your place among the faithful.	Invite reflection on belonging.
Catechetical Acclamation	This is the Church's faith, handed down through the ages and confessed among the saints. Amen.	Lead the acclamation reverently.

Catechetical Reception—Forgiveness of Sins

Function	Witness of the People of God by the Spirit	Instructor Cues
Proemial Orientation	Beloved catechumen, you are not invited here to weigh opinions or to devise a private account of mercy, but to receive what the Church has long spoken, prayed, enacted, and guarded concerning the forgiveness of sins, a gift handed on from the apostles and entrusted to the faithful as a living confession within the body of Christ.	Address as reception, not discovery.
Doctrinal Proposition Asserted	We acknowledge the forgiveness of sins, which God grants through Jesus Christ, by whom sins are remitted, consciences are cleansed, and persons are restored to communion with God and with the Church.	Invite memorization.
Diachronic Reception Anchoring	From the beginning, the Lord himself placed forgiveness upon the lips of his disciples as a rule of daily prayer, teaching them to say, "Forgive us our debts, as we also have forgiven our debtors" (Matthew 6:12), a word given in the context of the Lord's Prayer during his earthly ministry in the first century, whereby forgiveness was fixed not as an occasional abstraction but as a repeated, liturgical act shaping the life of the community, and received by the Church as a stable pattern of prayer that binds divine mercy and communal reconciliation together.	Emphasize prayer-rule.
	The Lord himself immediately fixed forgiveness as moral accountability within the community by declaring, "If you forgive others their trespasses, your heavenly Father will also forgive you; but if you do not forgive others… neither will your Father forgive your trespasses" (Matthew 6:14–15), a dominical clarification in the first century that bound the reception of divine mercy to enacted neighbor-love, so that the Church learned to treat forgiveness not as private relief but as a communal form in which love of God is shown by reconciliation with the neighbor.	Keep the moral logic tethered to worship: this is spoken as an immediate gloss on the prayer-rule.

The apostolic preaching further anchored forgiveness within repentance and proclamation, as the risen Christ commanded that "repentance for the forgiveness of sins should be preached in his name to all nations" (Luke 24:47), a commission spoken after the resurrection in the first century that clarified forgiveness as a gift mediated through Christ's name and mission, thereby stabilizing the doctrine as inseparable from the Church's kerygma and received as the normative content of apostolic preaching.

Link forgiveness to mission.

On the day of Pentecost this forgiveness was joined irrevocably to baptism, when Peter declared, "Repent and be baptized every one of you in the name of Jesus Christ for the forgiveness of your sins" (Acts 2:38), a first-century proclamation that fixed forgiveness within the initiatory rite of the Church, confirming that remission of sins is not merely announced but conferred, and this was preserved by the Church as a constitutive element of Christian entry.

Stress baptismal conferral.

And our Lord ordered the reception of forgiveness by binding it to reconciliation with the neighbor, teaching, "If you are offering your gift at the altar and remember that your brother has something against you, leave your gift there... first be reconciled to your brother" (Matthew 5:23–24), so that the Church learned to receive forgiveness not as a private absolution detached from communal repair, but as a reconciled form of life in which mercy from God is confessed and enacted through restored communion with others.

Stress as communion-restoring, not merely guilt-removing— forgiveness regulated at the altar.

The earliest catechetical witnesses describe baptism itself as the washing that effects this forgiveness, as Justin Martyr wrote, "We have received the washing of forgiveness of sins" (Justin Martyr, *First Apology* [*Apologia Prima*] 61), around the middle of the second century, explaining to catechumens and outsiders alike that forgiveness is ritually bestowed in baptism, thereby deepening the Church's shared memory that remission belongs to the sacramental life rather than to private sentiment.

Note initiatory context.

The Church also confessed that forgiveness remains available after baptism through repentance and confession, as taught in early exhortation, "If we confess our sins, he is faithful and righteous to forgive us our sins" (1 John 1:9), a first-century articulation that bound divine forgiveness to truthful confession, stabilizing the doctrine across time as God's faithful action received through ordered response, and received as a rule for ongoing ecclesial life.

Highlight confession.

And the Church habituated forgiveness through ordered confession and reconciliation before offering the sacrifice of praise (*Didache* 4.14; 14.1), so that repentance and restored communion became a repeated communal form rather than an exceptional event..

Stress habit and communal restoration.

This faith was finally fixed in the Church's common confession when baptismal symbols declared, "I believe in the forgiveness of sins," a clause attested in early Roman and regional creeds of the second and third centuries and later received in the confession, "one baptism for the forgiveness of sins" (Niceno-Constantinopolitan Creed, 381), whereby forgiveness was rendered non-optional, creedal, and universally binding as part of the Church's public faith under the guidance of the Holy Spirit.

Identify creedal fixation.

Illocutionary Clarification	When the Church says, "We acknowledge the forgiveness of sins," she performs not speculation but confession, publicly recognizing and assenting to a gift already given by God in Christ and enacted within her sacramental and communal life.	Name speech-act.
Interrogation (Question and Answer)	The instructor asks, "What do you acknowledge concerning sins?" and the catechumen replies, "I acknowledge the forgiveness of sins, which God grants through Jesus Christ."	Speak aloud.
Boundary Clarification Clause	This acknowledgment does not mean that sin is ignored, excused, or dissolved by human resolve, nor that forgiveness arises from inward feeling alone, but that remission is God's act in Christ, ordered within repentance, confession, and the life of the Church.	Exclude misunderstandings.
Formational & Existential Implication	By acknowledging the forgiveness of sins, the catechumen is formed to live neither in despair nor presumption, but in humble confidence, approaching God in repentance, remaining within the reconciled community, and trusting Christ as the faithful giver of mercy.	Shape disposition.
Catechetical Acclamation	This is the faith of the Church, the forgiveness of sins through Jesus Christ, and to this faith we say together, Amen.	Invite communal assent.

Catechetical Reception—Future Coming and Judgment

Function	Witness of the People of God by the Spirit	Instructor Cues
Proemial Orientation	Beloved catechumen, you are now instructed in the hope confessed by the Church concerning the consummation of all things, a teaching not devised by private reasoning but received and handed on in the Church's voice, proclaimed in Scripture, prayed in the liturgy, and sealed in the common confession of the faithful.	Address directly; situate within handed-on instruction.
Doctrinal Proposition Asserted	We believe that Jesus Christ will come again in glory to judge the living and the dead, and that his kingdom will have no end.	Invite memorization; maintain exact wording.
Diachronic Reception Anchoring	The prophetic vision of the Son of Man "coming with the clouds of heaven" and receiving a dominion that "shall not be destroyed" provided Israel's apocalyptic grammar for divine judgment and indestructible rule (Daniel 7:13–14), articulated in the Second Temple period amid persecution and hope, and received by the Church as the pattern by which Christ's future coming and everlasting kingdom were understood and irrevocably fixed within her expectation under God's guiding providence.	Note OT anchor; stress grammar of hope and rule.
	The royal oracle promising that of the Messiah's government "there will be no end" arose within Isaiah's proclamation to David's house in the eighth century before Christ (Isaiah 9:7), stabilizing the predicate of endless reign later fused into the Church's confession of Christ's kingdom, received as a divine assurance preserved in the Church's memory.	Emphasize "no end" predicate.
	The Lord himself taught vigilance concerning his return, declaring that the Son of Man will come at an hour unknown and that watchfulness is required (Matthew 24:42–44), a first-century dominical instruction that fixed expectation and sobriety as normative and was received communally as authoritative teaching.	Connect vigilance to expectation.
	Jesus joined his coming in glory inseparably to judgment when he taught that "the Son of Man comes in his glory… and he will judge" all nations (Matthew 25:31–32), an apostolic Gospel proclamation that stabilized the coupling of glorious appearing and universal judgment within the Church's confession.	Couple glory and judgment.

Apostolic preaching confessed Christ as the one "appointed... to judge the living and the dead" (Acts 10:42), a first-century kerygmatic formula that became a stable confessional cadence, received and transmitted as a norm of proclamation by the Church.	Highlight apostolic formula.
The apostolic charge naming Christ Jesus "who will judge the living and the dead at his appearing" (2 Timothy 4:1) further tightened the linkage of appearing and judgment in the Church's earliest teaching, received as a solemn and binding witness.	Reinforce appearing–judgment link.
The Eucharistic acclamation "Maranatha" and the prayer "Let grace come and this world pass away" expressed the Church's expectation of the Lord's coming within worship (*Didache* 10.6), a late first–early second century liturgical practice that habituated eschatological hope as performative prayer and was communally preserved.	Note liturgical formation.
Church order embedded readiness for the Lord's coming as a communal obligation, exhorting the faithful to be prepared because "our Lord will come" (*Didache* 16.1), and concluding with the public vision that "the world will see the Lord coming upon the clouds of heaven" (*Didache* 16.8), thereby narrating expectation as a fixed catechetical script received by the Church.	Connect discipline and public coming.
Post-apostolic preaching confessed Jesus Christ "as God and as the Judge of the living and the dead" (*Second Clement* [*Secunda Clementis*] 1.1), a mid-second-century homiletic stabilization that closely anticipates creedal language and was received without contest in the Church's proclamation.	Note near-creedal form.
Baptismal symbols in Rome confessed that Christ will come "to judge the living and the dead" (Old Roman Symbol), a formula likely originating in the second century and repeated at initiation, whose performative use at baptism fixed the clause as non-optional within ecclesial identity.	Stress baptismal performativity.
The ecumenical confession declared that Christ "will come again to judge the living and the dead" (Council of Nicaea, 325), elevating the clause to conciliar normativity and receiving it as binding for the whole Church.	Mark conciliar authority.

	The universal creed completed the confession by proclaiming that he "will come again in glory to judge the living and the dead, and his kingdom will have no end" (Niceno-Constantinopolitan Creed, 381), definitively fusing coming, judgment, and endless kingdom into a single confessional unit received and preserved by the Church across worship and catechesis.	Identify definitive formulation.
Illocutionary Clarification	When the Church says these words, she does not speculate about future events but confesses, proclaims, and bears witness, binding herself to the truth of Christ's promised appearing and judgment as an act of corporate faith.	Name the speech-act.
Interrogation (Question and Answer)	Question: What do you believe concerning Jesus Christ at the end of the age? Answer: I believe that he will come again in glory to judge the living and the dead, and that his kingdom will have no end.	Speak aloud; call-and-response.
Boundary Clarification Clause	This confession does not teach that the time of the Lord's coming is known, nor that his judgment is merely symbolic, nor that his kingdom is temporary or replaced, but it rejects all such misunderstandings by affirming a real coming, a true judgment, and an everlasting reign.	Clarify by exclusion.
Formational & Existential Implication	By this belief the catechumen is formed to live in watchful hope, to worship with expectation, and to order allegiance toward the coming Lord whose justice and mercy will be revealed, without confusing doctrine with moral calculation.	Orient life and worship.
Catechetical Acclamation	This is the faith of the Church, handed on from the apostles, confessed in baptism, proclaimed in the liturgy, and received by the faithful. Amen.	Conclude with communal assent.

Catechetical Reception—Life of the Age to Come

Function	Witness of the People of God by the Spirit	Instructor Cues
Proemial Orientation	Beloved catechumen, you are now instructed in the hope that the Church has received, guarded, and proclaimed from the beginning, not as a matter of private expectation but as a confession handed on in the communion of saints, wherein the living God addresses his people and binds them to the promise of what he himself will accomplish at the end of all things.	Emphasize reception and handing-on rather than speculation.
Doctrinal Proposition Asserted	We believe that God will raise the dead, granting the resurrection of the body and the life of the age to come, according to his power and faithfulness, as he has promised and as the Church confesses in hope.	Invite memorization of the core formula.
Diachronic Reception Anchoring	The Church first received this confession from the Lord himself, who taught that "all who are in the graves will hear his voice and come forth—those who have done good to the resurrection of life, and those who have done evil to the resurrection of condemnation" (John 5:28–29), spoken in the first century as part of the Gospel proclamation, thereby fixing within the Church's memory that the resurrection is God's act, universal in scope, bodily in character, and decisive for the age to come, a teaching received and preserved as normative under the guidance of the Holy Spirit.	Read slowly to underscore bodily resurrection.
	The Church also received the resurrection hope in Israel's apocalyptic confession that "many who sleep in the dust of the earth shall awake... some to everlasting life" (Daniel 12:2), a durable memory-form arising amid persecution that provided the Church with fixed language for bodily resurrection and the life of the age to come.	Stress continuity of hope; persecution-context strengthens reception.
	This apostolic teaching was further stabilized when Paul bore witness before rulers that "there will be a resurrection of the dead, both of the just and the unjust" (Acts 24:15), a first-century confession arising from missionary proclamation and public defense, which irreversibly established within the Church that no human life lies outside God's summons to resurrection, a conviction received across communities as part of the apostolic rule of faith.	Note universal scope without elaboration.

	The same hope was given concrete form when the Apostle taught that "the dead will be raised incorruptible, and this mortal must put on immortality" (1 Corinthians 15:52–53), written in the mid-first century to correct confusion among believers, thereby norming the Church's language of resurrection as bodily continuity transformed by God, a formulation preserved and transmitted as a non-negotiable confession of the Church's hope.	Stress continuity and transformation.
	In the earliest catechetical instruction, the Church taught the faithful to await "the resurrection of the dead" as a sign of truth when "the Lord shall come with all his saints" (*Didache* 16), composed at the turn of the first to second century for communal vigilance, thus embedding resurrection hope within lived expectation and confirming its place as a settled and teachable element of Christian formation.	Connect watchfulness to hope.
	This hope was compressed into baptismal confession when the Church came to say, "I look for the resurrection of the dead and the life of the age to come" (Niceno-Constantinopolitan Creed, 381), articulated in the context of conciliar settlement to safeguard the apostolic faith, thereby fixing this doctrine ecumenically and irreversibly as the Church's shared and public confession, received and guarded in unity by the whole body of Christ.	Identify this as the classic creedal form.
Illocutionary Clarification	When the Church says, "We believe" concerning the resurrection and the life of the age to come, she performs an act of confession and proclamation, binding herself publicly to God's promise and declaring her allegiance to the future he alone brings to fulfillment.	Clarify belief as enacted speech.
Interrogation (Question and Answer)	The instructor asks, "Do you believe that God will raise the dead and grant the life of the age to come?" The catechumen replies, "I believe that God will raise the dead and give the resurrection of the body and the life of the age to come."	Speak aloud in dialogical form.
Boundary Clarification Clause	This confession does not mean a mere survival of the soul apart from the body, nor a return to the present age, nor a hope secured by human effort, but the definitive act of God who raises the whole person and ushers creation into the age that has no end.	Guard against reduction or confusion.

Formational & Existential Implication	By receiving this faith, the catechumen is formed to live in hope rather than fear, to endure the present age without despair, and to belong wholly to God, knowing that life and death alike are held within his promise of resurrection and renewal.	Link hope to perseverance.
Catechetical Acclamation	This is the faith of the Church, this is the hope she proclaims, and in this confession we stand together, awaiting the resurrection of the dead and the life of the age to come. Amen.	Invite communal assent.

PART III.
PUBLIC WORSHIP

(LITURGY)

Liturgical Orientation:
Doctrinal Enactment

This faith is not only articulated by the Church but enacted by her. What the Church believes and confesses is received, rehearsed, stabilized, and handed on through her common worship, wherein the people of God are gathered before the Lord to hear his Word, to offer prayer and praise, and to participate in the holy mysteries entrusted to the Church. Doctrine is therefore not held in abstraction or merely spoken about, but spoken to God and enacted before God, embodied in ritual practice, and sustained within the life of the ecclesial community.

From the beginning, the Church has confessed the faith within her liturgy, prior to formal creedal definition, so that what is believed is prayed, and what is prayed is believed. Early Christian worship presupposed and transmitted a shared doctrinal core through baptismal confession, eucharistic thanksgiving, fasting, psalmody, and doxology, without recourse to speculative or philosophical explanation (*Didache* 7–10). In this way, the liturgy itself functioned as a *regula fidei* in action, receiving and safeguarding the apostolic faith through repeated communal enactment rather than discursive exposition (Irenaeus of Lyons, *Against Heresies* [*Adversus Haereses*] I.10).

Accordingly, the Articles of Faith are not merely statements about the faith but ecclesial acts by which the Church commits herself anew to the truth she has received. When used in worship, they function as corporate speech-acts— spoken in the first-person plural as acts of trust, allegiance, and thanksgiving— rather than as objects of explanation or analysis. Such use reflects the earliest pattern of Christian assembly, in which Scripture, prayer, Eucharist, and communal assent ("Amen") together constituted the Church's ratification of belief (Justin Martyr, *First Apology* [*Apologia Prima*] 65–67).

Liturgy is thus inherently doxological as well as confessional. What the Church believes, she also praises; and what she praises, she thereby confesses as true. Trinitarian doctrine, in particular, has been preserved and guarded not only by definition but by right praise, as the Church addresses glory to the Father, and to the Son, and to the Holy Spirit in psalms, hymns, and fixed doxologies (Basil of Caesarea, *On the Holy Spirit* [*De Spiritu Sancto*] 27). In such worship, theology is sung, prayed, and proclaimed as living truth, and orthodoxy is sustained by orthopathy no less than by formal articulation (Athanasius of Alexandria, *Letter to Marcellinus* [*Epistula ad Marcellinum*]).

At the same time, liturgy marks and maintains the boundaries of ecclesial life. The faith is confessed in order to enter, remain, and be nourished within the Church. Baptismal interrogations enact confession as a ritually consequential commitment, and Eucharistic communion presupposes and renews that confession within the gathered body (*Apostolic Tradition*; Cyril of Jerusalem, *Mystagogical Catecheses* [*Mystagogicae Catecheses*]). In this way, confession is not merely verbal but embodied, binding the Church to the faith she lives by and guarding it through participation rather than publication.

For this reason, the Church does not invent, revise, or expand her faith in worship. Rather, she bears faithful witness to the apostolic teaching by rehearsing it in prayer, thanksgiving, proclamation, and communal assent. The Articles may therefore be recited in whole or in part, placed alongside the proclamation of Scripture, or used at moments of baptismal renewal or festal emphasis, always without alteration. In such enactment, the confession is not explained or defended; it is entrusted to God and made audible as the unified voice of the Church.

Thus, this confession is inseparable from the Church's liturgical life and from her continuity across time. The faith is handed on not only by texts but by received forms of worship, whose stability bears witness to the Church's constancy of belief across generations. As the Church worships, so she believes; and as she believes, so she worships, offering herself in faithful obedience to the one God who has made himself known for our salvation.

Gathering and Invocation

When the Church is assembled, the liturgy begins with an invocation of the one God, by which the community is gathered not by human initiative but by divine call. The assembly confesses the name of the Lord and offers praise, thereby situating all that follows within the worship of the one God who is Father, Son, and Holy Spirit. This invocation establishes the ecclesial "We" as a worshiping body and commits the assembly to speak and act in fidelity to the faith it confesses.

Liturgy Spoken	Presider Marginalia
In the name of the one God, the LORD, who is and who was and who is to come.	May be spoken by the presider alone or intoned with the assembly responding "Amen." Establishes divine initiative.
We gather before you, O God, not by our own choosing, but by your call.	Frames the assembly as summoned, not self-constituted. Avoids voluntarism.
You are the Creator of heaven and earth, of all things visible and invisible.	Echoes Article II language; spoken slowly and clearly.
You have made us for yourself, and our life is found in you.	Anthropological grounding without later metaphysical terms.
We confess Jesus Christ, your Son, as our Lord,	Christological confession begins; slight pause recommended after "confess."
through whom you have made yourself known and through whom you have redeemed us.	Keeps incarnation and salvation implicit, not yet narrated.
We believe in the Holy Spirit, who gives life and gathers your people into one.	Pneumatological confession tied to ecclesial unity.
Therefore, as one body, we come before you in faith and obedience.	Explicitly constitutes the ecclesial "We."
Receive our worship, our confession, and our thanksgiving,	Tripartite offering: worship (doxology), confession (faith), thanksgiving (eucharistic horizon).
and order our hearts and words according to the truth you have entrusted to your Church.	Requests fidelity, not creativity; reinforces reception.
As we hear your Word and confess our faith,	Transitional line toward proclamation and creed.
bind us together in the unity of belief, hope, and love.	Triadic virtues without later scholastic framing.

Liturgy Spoken	Presider Marginalia
To you be glory, now and forever.	Doxological closure.
Amen.	Preferably spoken by the entire assembly.

Proclamation of the Word

The Scriptures are then read publicly, according to the ordered reading of the Church, so that the saving acts of God may be proclaimed before the people. Through the hearing of the Word, the assembly receives anew the testimony of the prophets and apostles concerning creation, redemption, resurrection, judgment, and the life of the age to come. The proclamation of Scripture is received not as private instruction but as a communal address, calling forth faith, obedience, and confession.

Following the reading, the Word may be expounded for the instruction of the faithful, so that the Church may understand more fully what she confesses and how she is to live in accordance with it. Such instruction serves the confession, but does not replace it.

Liturgy Spoken	Presider Marginalia
We believe in one God, the LORD, and we confess that there is no other.	Spoken by the entire assembly. Establishes monotheistic confession as foundational.
We believe that the one God is the Creator of heaven and earth, of all things visible and invisible.	Maintain steady pace; echoes creedal and doxological usage.
We confess Jesus Christ, God's Son, as our Lord.	Slight pause before and after "Jesus Christ." Central Christological confession.
We believe and confess that for us and for our salvation the Son of God, the Word, became flesh.	Commissive language ("for us") should be emphasized.
He was conceived by the Holy Spirit and born of the Virgin Mary.	Maintain sobriety of tone; avoid dramatization.
He suffered under Pontius Pilate, was crucified, died, and was buried.	Historical anchoring; speak plainly and clearly.
He descended to the dead.	Brief pause after the line; allow gravity without elaboration.
On the third day he rose bodily from the dead.	Emphasize "bodily" without additional explanation.
He appeared to witnesses, ascended into heaven, and is seated at the right hand of the Father.	Ascension and exaltation confessed as completed acts.
He will come again in glory to judge the living and the dead, and his kingdom will have no end.	Eschatological horizon; avoid haste.
We believe in the Holy Spirit, who gives life,	Begin pneumatological section with clarity.
who unites the Church and sanctifies the people of God.	Emphasizes ecclesial and sanctifying work.
We acknowledge one, holy, catholic, and apostolic Church.	"Catholic" to be spoken without qualification.
We acknowledge the forgiveness of sins, which God grants through Jesus Christ.	Soteriological reception stated, not mechanized.

We believe that God will raise the dead,

Begin resurrection confession with reverence.

granting the resurrection of the body and the life of the age to come.

Final eschatological promise; do not rush.

To this faith we commit ourselves,

Explicit commissive turn; may be spoken slightly louder.

receiving it as the faith handed down from the apostles.

Emphasizes reception, not innovation.

We confess this faith before God and the world,

Public and theocentric orientation.

and we resolve to live in obedience to it,

Ethical implication stated without moral enumeration.

until the Lord comes again.

Eschatological perseverance.

Amen.

Preferably spoken firmly by the entire assembly.

Corporate Confession of Faith

Having heard the Word, the assembly confesses the faith together in a unified voice. The articles of faith are spoken aloud as first-person plural declarations, by which the Church binds herself to the truth of what is confessed. In this act, the community does not merely affirm propositions, but publicly commits itself to the faith once delivered and to the life that flows from it.

This confession functions as an ecclesial act of fidelity, by which the Church bears witness before God and the world to what she believes, confesses, and holds. Through this common confession, the Church is ordered in unity, guarded against false teaching, and joined to the communion of the faithful across time and place.

Liturgy Spoken	Presider Marginalia
We believe in one God, the LORD, and we confess that there is no other.	Spoken by the entire assembly. Establishes monotheistic confession as foundational.
We believe that the one God is the Creator of heaven and earth, of all things visible and invisible.	Maintain steady pace; echoes creedal and doxological usage.
We confess Jesus Christ, God's Son, as our Lord.	Slight pause before and after "Jesus Christ." Central Christological confession.
We believe and confess that for us and for our salvation the Son of God, the Word, became flesh.	Commissive language ("for us") should be emphasized.
He was conceived by the Holy Spirit and born of the Virgin Mary.	Maintain sobriety of tone; avoid dramatization.
He suffered under Pontius Pilate, was crucified, died, and was buried.	Historical anchoring; speak plainly and clearly.
He descended to the dead.	Brief pause after the line; allow gravity without elaboration.
On the third day he rose bodily from the dead.	Emphasize "bodily" without additional explanation.
He appeared to witnesses, ascended into heaven, and is seated at the right hand of the Father.	Ascension and exaltation confessed as completed acts.
He will come again in glory to judge the living and the dead, and his kingdom will have no end.	Eschatological horizon; avoid haste.
We believe in the Holy Spirit, who gives life,	Begin pneumatological section with clarity.
who unites the Church and sanctifies the people of God.	Emphasizes ecclesial and sanctifying work.
We acknowledge one, holy, catholic, and apostolic Church.	"Catholic" to be spoken without qualification.

Liturgy Spoken	Presider Marginalia
We acknowledge the forgiveness of sins, which God grants through Jesus Christ.	Soteriological reception stated, not mechanized.
We believe that God will raise the dead,	Begin resurrection confession with reverence.
granting the resurrection of the body and the life of the age to come.	Final eschatological promise; do not rush.
To this faith we commit ourselves,	Explicit commissive turn; may be spoken slightly louder.
receiving it as the faith handed down from the apostles.	Emphasizes reception, not innovation.
We confess this faith before God and the world,	Public and theocentric orientation.
and we resolve to live in obedience to it,	Ethical implication stated without moral enumeration.
until the Lord comes again.	Eschatological perseverance.
Amen.	Preferably spoken firmly by the entire assembly.

Intercessory Prayer and Thanksgiving

Following the confession, the Church offers prayers of intercession and thanksgiving. In these prayers, the assembly entrusts itself, the world, and all creation to God, acknowledging dependence upon his mercy and governance. Thanksgiving is offered for the saving work of God in Christ and for the life given by the Holy Spirit, thereby reinforcing in prayer what has been confessed in word.

These prayers are not ancillary but integral to the confession, for they enact trust in the God whom the Church has confessed and express reliance upon his promises.

Liturgy Spoken	Presider Marginalia
Let us pray to the Lord.	Spoken by the presider; may be followed by silence.
O God, the Creator of all things,	Invocation recalls Article II; establishes universal scope.
you have made heaven and earth and sustain all that you have made.	Grounds prayer in divine providence, not human need alone.
We give you thanks for the gift of life,	Thanksgiving begins before petition, reflecting ancient pattern.
for the breath you place in every living thing,	Avoid poetic excess; steady cadence.
and for your mercy that endures through all generations.	Scriptural resonance without citation.
We thank you above all for Jesus Christ our Lord,	Christological thanksgiving anchors all petitions.
through whom you have reconciled the world to yourself.	Soteriology stated without theory.
By his death you have overcome sin,	Speak plainly; avoid dramatization.
and by his resurrection you have opened for us the way of life.	Resurrection framed as participatory promise.
We thank you for the Holy Spirit,	Pneumatological thanksgiving follows naturally.
who gives life to your people and gathers the Church in unity.	Ecclesial orientation emphasized.
Trusting in your mercy, we now bring before you our prayers.	Transition from thanksgiving to intercession.
Remember, O Lord, your holy Church throughout the world.	Ancient formula; universal intercession.
Preserve her in faith, hope, and love,	Theological virtues invoked without elaboration.

Liturgy Spoken	Presider Marginalia
and keep her steadfast in the truth entrusted to her.	Guards against innovation language.
Strengthen all who serve your people,	May include ordained and lay without specification.
that they may teach, shepherd, and lead in humility and faithfulness.	Functional, not hierarchical emphasis.
Remember the nations and all who govern them.	Civic intercession; pre-Constantinian compatible.
Grant wisdom to those in authority,	Avoid political specificity.
that peace may be upheld and justice pursued.	Broad moral goods only.
Remember those who suffer in body, mind, or spirit.	Inclusive suffering categories.
Give healing to the sick,	Short petitions preferred.
comfort to the sorrowful,	Maintain measured pace.
relief to the oppressed,	Social concern stated without ideology.
and hope to all who are in despair.	Eschatological orientation implicit.
Remember those who have died in the hope of the resurrection.	Avoid naming intermediate states.
Grant them rest in your peace,	Ancient phrasing; neutral across traditions.
and keep us in communion with all your saints.	Communal continuity across time.
As we have confessed the faith with our lips,	Explicit linkage to prior confession.
so order our lives according to your will.	Ethical implication without casuistry.
Make us faithful witnesses to your truth,	Missional but restrained.

Liturgy Spoken	Presider Marginalia
steadfast in obedience,	Commissive reinforcement.
and patient in hope,	Eschatological virtue.
until the day when Christ comes again in glory.	Final horizon; do not rush.
To you, O God, be thanks and praise,	Doxological turn.
now and forever.	Timeless orientation.
Amen.	Preferably spoken firmly by the entire assembly.

Eucharistic Thanksgiving

When the Church celebrates the thanksgiving over bread and wine, she proclaims the saving death and resurrection of the Lord and anticipates his coming in glory. In this act, the Church does not repeat the sacrifice of Christ but gives thanks for the once-for-all work accomplished for our salvation. The assembly participates in this thanksgiving as a sign of communion with Christ and with one another, confessing through action the faith proclaimed in words.

Participation in this thanksgiving presupposes the faith confessed and serves to strengthen the Church in fidelity to it.

Liturgy Spoken	Presider Marginalia
The Lord be with you.	Spoken by the presider. Ancient dialogical opening.
And with your spirit.	Spoken by the assembly. Maintain steady, unified response.
Lift up your hearts.	Presider invites the interior act of thanksgiving.
We lift them up to the Lord.	Assembly responds as one voice.
Let us give thanks to the Lord our God.	Invitation to eucharistic act proper.
It is right to give him thanks and praise.	Assembly affirms the fittingness of thanksgiving.
It is truly right and good to give you thanks,	Presider begins extended thanksgiving.
O God, the Father almighty,	Naming God without later metaphysical qualifiers.
the Creator of heaven and earth,	Echoes the confessed faith; slow and clear.
for you are the source of life and the giver of all good things.	Establishes divine generosity.
You formed humanity in your image,	Anthropological grounding without speculation.
and when we turned away, you did not abandon us,	Covenant faithfulness emphasized.
but in mercy you acted for our salvation.	Salvation framed as divine initiative.
You sent your Son, Jesus Christ our Lord,	Christological turn; pause after the name.
who for us and for our salvation became flesh,	Echoes prior confession; commissive language retained.

Liturgy Spoken	Presider Marginalia
suffered, died, and was raised from the dead,	Paschal sequence spoken plainly.
that we might have life and hope in him.	Soteriological telos stated simply.
Therefore, remembering his saving work,	Transition to anamnesis.
we give you thanks and proclaim your praise.	Thanksgiving and proclamation united.
In the night in which he was handed over,	Institution narrative begins; solemn pace.
our Lord Jesus Christ took bread,	Do not embellish gesture; clarity preferred.
gave thanks, broke it, and gave it to his disciples, saying:	Maintain continuity of action verbs.
"Take and eat; this is my body, given for you. Do this in remembrance of me."	Speak the words distinctly; allow silence after.
In the same way, after supper, he took the cup,	Resume with calm cadence.
gave thanks, and gave it to them, saying:	Parallel structure preserved.
"Drink from it, all of you; this is my blood of the covenant, poured out for you and for many for the forgiveness of sins. Do this, as often as you drink it, in remembrance of me."	Avoid explanatory additions.
Therefore, as we remember his death and resurrection,	Anamnesis continues.
we offer you this thanksgiving,	"Offer" refers to thanksgiving, not repetition.
proclaiming the mystery of faith:	Optional acclamation cue.
Christ has died. Christ is risen. Christ will come again.	May be spoken by all or by presider.
Send now your Holy Spirit upon your people,	Epiclesis directed to the assembly first.
that we may receive these gifts in faith,	Avoid mechanistic language.

Liturgy Spoken	Presider Marginalia
and be united as one body in Christ.	Ecclesial effect emphasized.
Make us a living offering of praise,	Ethical and doxological turn.
faithful in hope and steadfast in love,	Virtue language maintained.
until the day when he comes again in glory.	Eschatological horizon reaffirmed.
Through him, with him, and in him,	Doxological ascent.
to you, O God, be glory and honor,	God-ward orientation explicit.
now and forever.	Timeless closure.
Amen.	Preferably sung or spoken firmly by the entire assembly.

Doxology and Sending

The liturgy concludes with praise and doxology, by which glory is ascribed to God alone. In offering praise, the Church confesses that all truth, salvation, and life belong to God, and that the faith she has confessed is ordered toward his glory.

The assembly is then sent forth into the world, having committed itself anew to the faith it has confessed. This sending signifies that the confession enacted in worship is to be lived out in obedience, witness, and love, until the Lord comes again.

Liturgy Spoken	Presider Marginalia
Let us give glory to God.	Spoken by the presider; invites unified doxology.
We give glory to God alone.	Assembly responds; affirms divine exclusivity.
Glory be to the Father,	Begin Trinitarian doxology; steady, unhurried pace.
and to the Son,	Maintain parallel structure; avoid added emphasis.
and to the Holy Spirit,	Completes Trinitarian naming without explanation.
as it was in the beginning,	Temporal continuity emphasized.
is now,	Present participation.
and will be forever.	Eschatological permanence.
Amen.	Spoken by all; may be sung or spoken.
Having given thanks and confessed our faith,	Presider resumes; transitional statement.
let us now be sent forth in peace.	Peace as condition for mission.
The Lord has spoken;	Word-centered authority, not clerical.
let us be faithful in obedience.	Commissive implication stated plainly.
Go forth as witnesses to the truth you have confessed,	Mission flows directly from confession.
living in faith, hope, and love.	Virtue triad reiterated.
Serve the Lord in the unity of the Spirit,	Pneumatological grounding for mission.
and in communion with the whole Church.	Ecclesial continuity affirmed.

Liturgy Spoken	Presider Marginalia
May the blessing of the one God be upon you,	Optional blessing; remains non-rite-specific.
who is Father, Son, and Holy Spirit.	Trinitarian naming retained.
Now and forever.	Timeless scope of blessing.
Amen.	Spoken firmly by the entire assembly.

PART IV.
PROFESSIONAL STANDARD

(ECCLESIA)

Communal Orientation:
Doctrinal Statements

From the fourth century onward, professions of faith functioned not only as catechetical summaries or liturgical recitations, but as normative instruments of ecclesial order. Once articulated in common form, the confession of faith became a shared measure by which communion was recognized, teaching was bounded, and leadership was held accountable. This development did not arise from speculative systematization, but from the Church's need to preserve unity of confession across persons, offices, and communities.

The earliest ecumenical councils provide direct evidence of this function. At the Council of Nicaea (325), the creed was not merely proclaimed but subscribed by bishops, with refusal resulting in deposition and exile, and reconciliation later conditioned upon renewed subscription (Eusebius of Caesarea, *Life of Constantine* III.23–24). The confession thus served as an office-binding standard, establishing doctrinal adherence as a condition of ecclesial authority.

This confessional standard was also subject to canonical enforcement. The Nicene settlement was accompanied by conciliar canons and imperial edicts that imposed penalties for doctrinal nonconformity, including banishment and exclusion from ecclesial recognition (Council of Nicaea, Creed and Canons, 325; Constantine's edicts against Arius and his followers). Under Theodosius I, imperial legislation explicitly identified adherence to the Trinitarian confession as the criterion for being named "Catholic Christians," while alternative doctrines were legally stigmatized as heretical (Theodosius I, *Cunctos Populos*, 380). In this context, the profession of faith functioned as a public and enforceable boundary of communal identity.

By the fifth century, the Church further clarified the institutional finality of the received confession. The Council of Ephesus (431) formally prohibited the composition, promulgation, or public use of "another creed" beyond that of Nicaea, forbidding not only contradiction but also supplementation (Council of Ephesus, Canon 7). This prohibition established an institution-wide rule against doctrinal alternatives, locating the authority of the confession in its reception by the Church rather than in the creativity of later teachers or assemblies.

These same sources demonstrate that the confession served as a rule-governed standard of leadership accountability. Bishops were judged, condemned, deposed, or restored by reference to their conformity to the received faith, rather than by appeal to personal authority or local custom (Acts of the Council of Nicaea, 325; Acts of the Council of Ephesus, 431). The creed thus functioned as an external and shared measure to which even the highest ecclesial offices were subject.

What emerges from this pre-Schism evidence is a consistent pattern: once a confession was received by the Church in common, it became normative without being exhaustive, authoritative without being speculative, and binding without being innovative. Its authority lay not in continuous reinterpretation, but in faithful reception and public assent.

The forms of confessional use that developed—liturgical, catechetical, conciliar, juridical, and institutional—were not competing functions, but contextual applications of a single received confession. Communities did not alter the content of the faith to suit different uses; rather, they clarified the *manner* in which the same confession governed worship, teaching, office, and cooperation.

The sections that follow generalize these historically attested patterns in a disciplined way. They do not expand the Articles of Faith, nor do they prescribe a single mode of adoption. Instead, they provide normed forms by which churches, institutions, and associations may recognizably receive the confession—publicly, formally, and without alteration—according to their proper vocation and structure, in continuity with the Church's earlier practice.

Placement and Use Guidance

This section is to be situated immediately prior to the Articles of Faith, serving as the final orienting material before the confession itself is presented. Its purpose is not to interpret, qualify, or supplement the Articles, but to clarify the manner and scope of their formal reception by different kinds of communities, in continuity with the Church's historical practice.

Communities may receive the Articles in either a minimal or expanded form of attestation. A minimal stance records only the fact of reception and should employ the **Minimal Attestation of Reception** provided.

An expanded stance may articulate how the received confession functions within the community's life, governance, teaching, or cooperation, provided that such articulation does not alter, restate, or extend the doctrinal content of the Articles themselves.

Once the Articles of Faith are set forth, they should stand without commentary, annotation, or appended doctrinal explanation. Historically, the authority of a received confession has resided in its public articulation and communal assent, not in surrounding interpretive scaffolding.

Any expansion of the Articles to denote denominational or contextual distinctives must therefore, in a separate location and manner, elaborate the Articles and never contravene nor redefine these essential beliefs.

If a community wishes to record formal assent, a signature or attestation page may follow the Articles. Such a page should be administrative in character, recording reception and subscription without paraphrasing, summarizing, or supplementing the confession.

Whether minimal or expanded language precedes the Articles, the confession itself concludes the doctrinal content of the document; any subsequent material exists solely to witness to its reception.

Churches, Congregations, Communions

Ecclesial Reception

When received by a church or ecclesial body, the Articles serve as a rule of common confession. They articulate the faith publicly held and spoken by the community in worship, sacrament, catechesis, and discipline, and they establish the doctrinal horizon within which Scripture is read, preached, and obeyed.

In this form of reception, the Articles function as an office-binding and membership-defining standard. They may be referenced in matters of teaching responsibility, pastoral oversight, admission to ministry, and ecclesial accountability. Their authority derives not from local preference, but from their continuity with the Church's received confession.

(Church or Congregation)

Confessional Statement

We, the members of **[Name of Church]**, receiving the faith handed down in the Church from the beginning, hereby affirm and adopt the *Articles of Faith* as a true and faithful confession of the Christian faith.

These Articles are received as the common confession of this church, governing our proclamation, worship, catechesis, and the exercise of ecclesial office. They do not replace Holy Scripture, nor do they exhaust the mystery of the faith, but they name the shared doctrinal horizon within which Scripture is read, preached, and obeyed among us.

In matters of teaching, leadership, and ecclesial accountability, the Articles shall serve as a normative reference, binding us only where the Church has long spoken with one voice.

Adopted by **[Governing Body]** on **[Date]**.

Universities, Schools, Ministries, Charities

Institutional Adoption

When received by an institution, the Articles function as a confessional standard of identity and accountability. They define the doctrinal commitments under which the institution understands its mission, governance, instruction, and public representation.

In this form, the confession governs institutional self-understanding, not sacramental life. It establishes the theological boundaries within which teaching, scholarship, formation, and service are carried out, without prescribing uniformity of method, disciplinary approach, or secondary theological opinion beyond what is explicitly confessed.

Such reception provides a stable doctrinal reference that can be publicly named, formally affirmed, and responsibly relied upon in matters of leadership, employment, and institutional trust.

(University, School, Ministry, or Charitable Body)

Doctrinal Identity Statement

[Name of Institution] affirms and adopts the *Articles of Faith* as its confessional standard, expressing the doctrinal commitments under which it understands its mission, governance, instruction, and public witness.

The Articles are received as written, as a coherent whole, and as sufficient for identifying the center of belief that informs the institution's work. This adoption establishes a common doctrinal horizon while permitting diversity of scholarly method, pedagogical approach, and disciplinary specialization, provided such work remains within the bounds of the confession received.

Nothing in this adoption requires assent to theological positions not expressly confessed in the Articles, nor does it foreclose responsible inquiry conducted in continuity with them.

Adopted by [Board / Authority] on [Date].

Networks, Partnerships, Societies, Alliances

Associational or Cooperative Reception

When received by an association or cooperative body, the Articles serve as a basis for recognition and cooperation. They identify a shared confession sufficient for collaboration while deliberately refraining from governance over member bodies.

In this form, the Articles function as a marker of ecclesial proximity, enabling mutual trust, shared work, and public alignment without superseding the confessional documents, polity, or practices proper to each participating body.

The confession is thus acknowledged rather than administered: it binds cooperation without dissolving difference.

Statement of Common Confession

The undersigned bodies acknowledge the *Articles of Faith* as a faithful articulation of the Christian confession received by the Church across time and place, and recognize them as a sufficient basis for cooperation and shared witness.

This acknowledgment establishes a common confessional reference for collaboration while expressly preserving the autonomy, governance, confessional documents, and practices proper to each participating body. It does not authorize adjudication of internal doctrinal disputes nor impose uniformity beyond the shared confession acknowledged.

Endorsed on **[Date]**.

Minimal Attestation of Reception

Any Group Structure

A minimal attestation of reception is a public acknowledgment that a community has received a confession of faith as written. It does not create the confession, explain it, or add to it. It simply records that the community now stands under it.

Historically, when the Church received a creed or confession, what mattered was not repetition or elaboration, but recognizable assent. The attestation is the formal trace of that assent—identifying who has received the confession, in what capacity, and at what time.

For this reason, the attestation is intentionally brief. The confession itself states what is believed; the attestation only witnesses that it has been received and now governs the community's life or cooperation according to its form of reception.

By limiting itself to acknowledgment "as written," the attestation preserves the distinction between confession and interpretation and protects the confession from quiet modification over time. In short, a minimal attestation is the community's way of saying: this confession has been received, and we now stand under it.

Attestation of Reception

The undersigned hereby attest that the foregoing *Articles of Faith* have been received and affirmed **as written**, without alteration, supplementation, or abridgment, according to the form of confessional reception stated herein.

This attestation records an act of communal assent and bears witness to the public reception of the confession; it does not add to, interpret, or modify the Articles themselves.

Name of Body: _____
Form of Reception: _____
Authorizing Body or Officer: _____
Date of Reception: _____
Signature(s): _____

On The Stability and Use of This Edition
(Colophon)

This Statement of Faith is presented as a complete and self-contained confession of the Church's common faith, ordered for clarity, public reference, and faithful use. The Articles set forth herein are not provisional, nor are they intended for ongoing revision or expansion. They are offered as a settled witness to what the Church has long confessed together across time, place, and voice.

The text is published under an open license to encourage broad use, citation, and reproduction in ecclesial, educational, and institutional settings, provided that it is transmitted in its unaltered form and with appropriate attribution. Such use does not require endorsement of any particular body, nor does it imply submission to an external authority, but signifies continuity with the faith here confessed.

Future editions, should they be issued, will be identified solely by paratextual revision, typographic refinement, or contextual framing, and not by alteration of the doctrinal substance of the Articles or their concise summary. In this way, the integrity of the confession is preserved while its accessibility may be extended.

This Statement is offered to the Church not as a terminus, but as a measure: a stable reference by which belief may be articulated, taught, prayed, and affirmed, and by which unity of confession may be recognized without constraint of conscience beyond what has been received in common.

Rule of Faith
(Delimiting the Confession)

The faith confessed in this Statement is bounded not by private interpretation, local custom, or later speculation, but by the rule of faith received by the Church from the beginning. This rule does not exhaust the mystery of God, nor does it resolve every question that may arise in theology, devotion, or practice. Rather, it marks the contours within which the Church has recognized the gospel as the same gospel, confessed everywhere and always, even as it has been spoken in many tongues and lived in diverse contexts.

Accordingly, this Statement is not intended to function as a comprehensive system of doctrine, nor as a catalogue of all matters upon which Christians may rightly reflect or disagree. It is deliberately limited to those affirmations that have proven necessary for the coherence of the apostolic proclamation and the unity of ecclesial confession.

This rule of faith operates as a measure, not a mechanism. It names what the Church has already received, confessed, and practiced in common. Where it is honored, diversity of theological reflection may flourish without dissolving unity of confession. Where it is displaced, clarity gives way to fragmentation, and the common voice of faith is obscured.

Within this boundary, the Church speaks with confidence; beyond it, she speaks with humility or remains silent. Such restraint is not a failure of courage, but an expression of fidelity. The rule of faith guards the gospel not by multiplying definitions, but by preserving the integrity of what has been handed on.

Doxology

To the one God,
the LORD, the God of Israel,
the Father of our Lord Jesus Christ;

to the Son,
the Word made flesh for us and for our salvation,
who suffered, died, and was raised from the dead;

and to the Holy Spirit,
the giver of life,
who calls, sustains, and sanctifies the Church—

be glory, honor, and praise,
now and unto the ages of ages.
Amen.

Made in the USA
Columbia, SC
19 January 2026

77419418R00059